Cambridge Elements

Elements in Bioethics and Neuroethics
edited by
Thomasine Kushner
California Pacific Medical Center, San Francisco

ANTINATALISM, EXTINCTION, AND THE END OF PROCREATIVE SELF-CORRUPTION

Matti Häyry
Aalto University School of Business

Amanda Sukenick
The Exploring Antinatalism Podcast

Shaftesbury Road, Cambridge CB2 8EA, United Kingdom

One Liberty Plaza, 20th Floor, New York, NY 10006, USA

477 Williamstown Road, Port Melbourne, VIC 3207, Australia

314–321, 3rd Floor, Plot 3, Splendor Forum, Jasola District Centre,
New Delhi – 110025, India

103 Penang Road, #05–06/07, Visioncrest Commercial, Singapore 238467

Cambridge University Press is part of Cambridge University Press & Assessment,
a department of the University of Cambridge.

We share the University's mission to contribute to society through the pursuit of
education, learning and research at the highest international levels of excellence.

www.cambridge.org
Information on this title: www.cambridge.org/9781009455282

DOI: 10.1017/9781009455299

© Matti Häyry and Amanda Sukenick 2024

This publication is in copyright. Subject to statutory exception and to the provisions of relevant collective licensing agreements, with the exception of the Creative Commons version the link for which is provided below, no reproduction of any part may take place without the written permission of Cambridge University Press & Assessment.

An online version of this work is published at doi.org/10.1017/9781009455299 under a Creative Commons Open Access license CC-BY-NC 4.0 which permits re-use, distribution and reproduction in any medium for non-commercial purposes providing appropriate credit to the original work is given and any changes made are indicated. To view a copy of this license visit https://creativecommons.org/licenses/by-nc/4.0

When citing this work, please include a reference to the DOI 10.1017/9781009455299

First published 2024

A catalogue record for this publication is available from the British Library.

ISBN 978-1-009-45528-2 Hardback
ISBN 978-1-009-45530-5 Paperback
ISSN 2752-3934 (online)
ISSN 2752-3926 (print)

Cambridge University Press & Assessment has no responsibility for the persistence or accuracy of URLs for external or third-party internet websites referred to in this publication and does not guarantee that any content on such websites is, or will remain, accurate or appropriate.

Every effort has been made in preparing this Element to provide accurate and up-to-date information that is in accord with accepted standards and practice at the time of publication. Although case histories are drawn from actual cases, every effort has been made to disguise the identities of the individuals involved. Nevertheless, the authors, editors, and publishers can make no warranties that the information contained herein is totally free from error, not least because clinical standards are constantly changing through research and regulation. The authors, editors, and publishers therefore disclaim all liability for direct or consequential damages resulting fromthe use ofmaterial contained in this Element. Readers are strongly advised to pay careful attention to information provided by the manufacturer of any drugs or equipment that they plan to use.

Antinatalism, Extinction, and the End of Procreative Self-Corruption

Elements in Bioethics and Neuroethics

DOI: 10.1017/9781009455299
First published online: February 2024

Matti Häyry
Aalto University School of Business

Amanda Sukenick
The Exploring Antinatalism Podcast

Author for correspondence: Matti Häyry, matti.hayry@aalto.fi

Abstract: This Element provides an exploration of antinatalism, the view that assigns a negative value to reproduction. Section 1 traces the history of Western philosophy as a two-and-a-half millennia reaction to antinatalist sentiments. Human life has no obvious meaning and philosophers have been forced to build elaborate theories to invent imaginary purposes. Section 2 analyzes the concept of antinatalism in the light of human extinction. If people stop having children, the species will cease to exist, and this prospect has prompted attempts to find alternatives and excuses. Section 3 outlines a normative view, defending antinatalism both theoretically and practically. If it is wrong to bring about suffering in the absence of redeeming meaning and if it is possible to create meaning only by imposing a pronatalist mentality upon children before they can make up their own minds, parents morally corrupt themselves by procreating. This title is also available as Open Access on Cambridge Core.

This element also has a video abstract: Cambridge.org/EBAN_Hayry_abstract

Keywords: antinatalism, extinction, bioethics, pronatalism, meaning

© Matti Häyry and Amanda Sukenick 2024

ISBNs: 9781009455282 (HB), 9781009455305 (PB), 9781009455299 (OC)
ISSNs: 2752-3934 (online), 2752-3926 (print)

Contents

	Introduction	1
1	Western Philosophy as a Struggle against Antinatalism	4
2	Antinatalism and Extinction	25
3	Procreative Self-Corruption	42
	Notes	59
	References	64

Introduction

> The Greeks knew the terrors and horrors of existence, but they covered them with a veil in order to be able to live.
> — Friedrich Nietzsche, *The Birth of Tragedy*[1]

Antinatalism is a way of thinking and acting that has no universally accepted definition. Surface net sources like Wikipedia in English have had it that it is a "philosophical position that assigns a negative value judgement to birth and views procreation as immoral."[2] No major English dictionaries cover the term but two established French ones, *Larousse* and *Le Robert*, define "antinataliste" as an adjective and noun meaning "Qui vise à réduire la natalité" and "Qui cherche à limiter la natalité" – who or which aims to reduce or limit natality.[3] *Le Robert* further connects the word to Malthusian population policies.

Wikipedia entries can be biased, unreliable, and, in the case of contemporary movements, in a constant state of flux due to internal feuds within their memberships, but the moral wrongness of reproduction seems to be at the core of at least most academic attempts to analyze and assess antinatalism. *Larousse* and *Le Robert*'s focus is at the level of populations and population control, which reflects the often disparaging usage of the word in the French language and, in our experience, also in Latin America and Finland. These two characterizations are hardly exhaustive, but their similarities and differences will come in handy when we proceed to more explicit definitions.

As already seen in the *Le Robert* reference to Malthusian thinking, antinatalism can be conceptually, morally, ideologically, and politically connected to other "isms" and practices. These include (alphabetically and among others) abortion, altruism, animal rights, atheism, ecology, egoism, environmentalism, euthanasia, extinctionism, machine consciousness, natalism, neocolonialism, nihilism, pessimism, promortalism, pronatalism, suicide, and veganism. The justifications presented for antinatalism offer a wide range, too. Population growth degrades the natural environment. The world is a bad place and should not be more populated. Reproduction requires sex and sex is a sin. Our children's lives would be bad. We do not have their permission to bring them into existence. Life is suffering and we should not contribute to its continuation. Children are a burden. Children are a nuisance. Men are evil. Women are evil. Human beings are evil. Humankind inflicts suffering on other species. My life sucks. I wish I were dead. I wish I had never been born. My life has no meaning. Human life has no meaning. Life has no meaning. And to these we can add a plethora of religions and schools of thought. It is, to say the least, a mixed bag.

Our aim is to bring clarity to all this in three simple stages. The first (Section 1) is to show how ideas related to antinatalism have been expressed in European thinking and its predecessors since Greek Antiquity, and how some of the major philosophies in the West can be seen as pronatalist attempts to suppress and counteract emerging antinatalist tendencies. This is an interpretation that puts the shoe on the other foot. The prevailing consensus has been that antinatalist sentiments have been gradually brought to light by ever-evolving forms of Western philosophy. While this may be partially true, the wider truth is quite the opposite. The basic tenets of antinatalism have been known to thinking individuals for millennia, but every time they have threatened to disturb hegemonic establishments they have been crushed by philosophical systems such as those of Plato, Augustine of Hippo, and others. This is a bold hypothesis, but we believe that we can lend it some surprisingly credible support.

At the second stage of our presentation (Section 2), we shall cut through the layers of "isms" contemporarily associated with antinatalism by using, as a lens, extinctionism. The undeniable truth is that if no one has children, humankind will eventually die out. Doctrines that claim to be antinatalist have taken conflicting approaches to this matter, leaving both academics and the budding social movement perplexed and uncertain of what exactly is being promoted. Some so-called conditional versions of the creed have retracted from the extinctionist conclusion and settled for temporary or directed condemnations of reproduction. Without claiming linguistic authority on the definition, we argue that these philosophies could best be called selective pronatalism. We further argue that voluntary extinction of the species, understood correctly against current ethical ideals, should not jar our sensitivities excessively. This is another bold claim, but one that we trust we can make comprehensible and relatively palatable.

The third stage of our presentation (Section 3) takes us back to the beginning and demonstrates that one of the earliest recorded antinatalist attitudes may, with interim scientific and political developments, have come of age and may now be ready to serve the emerging social movement that questions the practice of reproduction. In the historical part of our narrative, we have identified the quest of meaning in life as the constant driving force of antinatalism. It has been muffled and stalled by influential Western philosophies but it has also gathered momentum through other advances in thinking and human interaction. Our argument, in all its simplicity, is that near-universal meaning in life can be secured, but only by imposing a pronatalist lifestyle upon new individuals in a manipulative way that we should no longer consider attractive, or acceptable. This, instead of the currently popular arguments from poor quality of all life (unconvincing), asymmetry of good and bad (incomprehensible), and lack of consent (complicated), would provide practical antinatalists, including artists and activists, with a relatable reason for not having children and proposing the same to others.

We opened this Introduction with a quote from Friedrich Nietzsche declaring that "The Greeks knew the terrors and horrors of existence, but they covered them with a veil in order to be able to live." We believe that he was on to something here and we add some key observations to his.

Not only the ancient Greeks but all thinking members of European societies have known the "terrors and horrors of existence," such as they are. Their reactions to these, as far as we can see, have depended on their underlying views on the meaning of life. The realization that there is no cosmic, ordained purpose has led people to philosophical pessimism; to concentration on the small, concrete pleasures in life; and, gradually, to antinatalist convictions. Insisting that there must be an overarching, universal purpose, on the other hand, has prompted thinkers to create complex, belief-defying edifices that explain the world and humankind's role in it in terms of divine order, afterlife, philosophical or political optimism, and eventually explicit pronatalism. This is the story of Western philosophy as a series of reactions to meaning-related challenges, in the service of traditional power structures. It is the story told in Section 1 of this Element – "Western Philosophy as a Struggle against Antinatalism."

In addition to the "terrors and horrors of existence," the fear of nonexistence has played an increasing part in reactions against antinatalist sentiments. This is especially true of philosophical considerations of the last few decades. A prominent ethical theory, utilitarianism, has slid into relative disgrace, in part because some of its versions can be associated with humankind's obligatory demise. According to negative utilitarianism, suffering should be minimized, maybe eliminated altogether, and what better way of accomplishing this than to end sentient, including human, life entirely? To a considerable degree, this is the question that defines the competing forms of antinatalist philosophy today. The distinctions that it forces and the specifications that answer to it make up the story of the varieties of contemporary antinatalism. It is the story told in Section 2 of this Element – "Antinatalism and Extinction."

Quoting Nietzsche one more time, while both negative utilitarians and their critics are well aware of the "terrors and horrors of existence," only the critics, like the Greeks and many others throughout the history of Western thought, have "covered them with a veil in order to be able to live." The veil has always consisted of a meta-narrative of life's universal meaning. The hardships are not denied but they are justified by an account of a higher purpose, first cosmic and divine, then more and more this-worldly. With secularization, technological advances, and an increasing awareness of the importance of freedom and happiness, we may have now reached pronatalism's last line of defense. It is that reproduction gives our lives meaning. And it does, but not spontaneously.

Our existence as reproducers has purpose only if we are manipulated into thinking so before we can freely form our own ideas of happiness and life goals. This, and its contradiction with widespread ethical ideals, is the story told in Section 3 of this Element – "Procreative Self-Corruption."

But enough of these abstract sketches of what we are going to say and onwards to saying it, with only these methodological notes beforehand. Our approach is that of applied moral and political philosophy. We seek evidence of sentiments, lines of thinking, arguments, and theories that touch upon antinatalist and related themes; expose connections; and weave a picture of how the philosophy and the movement have, or may have, developed during the millennia from Greek Antiquity to the present day. Our inferences aspire to be conceptually consistent and coherent, but we do not claim universal validity or soundness to our conclusions. Too many steps along the way are positional readings acceptable to thinking people with temperaments and worldviews matching ours, yet unacceptable to thinking people with different attitudes and background beliefs. Our findings take the form of assertive hypothetical – rather than categorical – imperatives. If and when our premises and deductions sound plausible, probably our conclusions should be taken seriously, too. But on to the story.

1 Western Philosophy as a Struggle against Antinatalism

The history of antinatalism is an elusive concept, not least because the doctrine and sentiment can be defined in many ways. In the Introduction, we listed a plethora of "isms," attitudes, phenomena, and arguments that could be chronologically cataloged; and Karim Akerma,[4] Kateřina Lochmanová,[5] Théophile de Giraud,[6] Masahiro Morioka,[7] Ramesh Mishra (under the pseudonym Ken Coates),[8] and others have done just that, all from their own points of view. It is not our intention to replicate this work.

We give structure to our own narrative by focusing mainly on the lack of meaning in human life; and on European attempts to come to terms with this. When related considerations emerge, they are duly noted and their links to contemporary antinatalism recorded.

By meaning we suggest a higher purpose or goal or a part to be played in some larger-than-us plan. The desire for this kind of meaning is by no means self-evident. People living ordinary lives are seldom preoccupied by the idea of a wider purpose, when all the guidance and consolation they need can be found in daily routines and social expectations. For some reason, however, the longing for something more has been present in Western thinking at least since the seventh century BCE. Life has its hardships – or, more dramatically, life is suffering – but this could be tolerable if we knew that those hardships are meaningful in an objective, universal way. Something in ancient Greek thought seems to have shaken the belief that the humanlike Olympian gods could guarantee such meaningfulness.[9] The doubt has persisted among thinking individuals throughout the centuries.

1.1 First Alarm: Scientific Worldview and Aversion to Children

An early yearning for meaning is indirectly expressed in the mythical character of Silenus, tutor and companion of the Greek wine god Dionysius. Silenus, a minor god himself, drowned his sorrows in wine and sex, only to find in his more sober moments that there was nothing in life to hold him, or anyone else for that matter, in its grip. In a quote from Aristotle preserved to us by Plutarch, Silenus reluctantly answers a question posed to him by King Midas about what is valuable in life:

> Ephemeral offspring of a travailing genius and of harsh fortune, why do you force me to speak what it were better for you men not to know?
>
> For a life spent in ignorance of one's own woes is most free from grief. But for men it is utterly impossible that they should obtain the best thing of all, or even have any share in its nature (for the best thing for all men and women is not to be born); however, the next best thing to this, and the first of those to which man can attain, but nevertheless only the second best, is, after being born, to die as quickly as possible.[10]

How should this be interpreted? A rash modern antinatalist could zoom in on the best-not-to-be-born part and say that ancient Greeks wanted to stop reproduction immediately. A promortalist – one who favors death over life – could pick up the last words, about dying as quickly as possible. These do not, however, exhaust the possibilities.

Starting the reading from the beginning, the text says that it is better not to know about life's true value because it has none, as a thinking person would be aware. It has woes and grief but no redeeming meaning. This is why it would be best not to be. But where should we go from here? Did the ancient Greeks, through their folklore, send us a message of pessimism and nihilism? Did they advise us to cease childbearing and to kill ourselves? That is doubtful, but what we can deduce is that such notions were known to them, ready to be linked with other views, possibly in combinations that would have the potential to challenge traditions and authorities.

The Wisdom of Silenus, as it is known in the literature, had expressions that well-preceded Aristotle, notably in the elegies of Theognis of Megara and the tragedies of Sophocles and Euripides;[11] and life's meaning apart from the wonders of the sky and the stars, the moon and the sun was questioned by

Anaxagoras,[12] all in the fifth and sixth centuries BCE. As for themes pertaining more directly to modern antinatalism, Thales of Miletus, of the sixth century BCE, is credited as the first pre-Socratic philosopher to say that to love one's children means not having them.[13] We have not included all the relevant quotes here but we have created an openly accessible repository where all the fragments and their sources can be found.[14]

While we identify the lack of meaning in life as the driving force of our story, we also recognize that it is always amplified by some other developments in thinking or social arrangements. In the case of the first antinatalist alarm, as we call it, the amplification comes from the scientific worldview and the apparent aversion to children that can be found in Democritus, the founder of the atomistic school.[15] The core of his teaching was that this world is composed of matter, or, to be more precise, small, invisible and indivisible particles that come together to form the visible and divisible objects that we can perceive. It is easy for us to relate to this theory because it is, essentially, the foundation of our own current worldview, give or take that our atoms can be further divided. Plato and Aristotle later took issue with the view in what, in our parlance, is the first reaction to the antinatalist alarm.

The textual evidence of Democritus' thought is indirect and uncertain, but these fragments, if reliable, give some clues at least to what others have seen him as advocating: "To bring up children is perilous; success is full of trouble and care, failure is unsurpassed by any other pain."[16] And, " I think that one should not have children; for in the having of children I see many great dangers, many pains, few advantages – and those thin and weak."[17] Thus, "Anyone who has a need for children would do better, I think, to get them from his friends. He will then have the child he wishes – for he can choose the sort he wants, and one that seems suitable to him will by its nature best follow him."[18]

The antinatalist could, again, hail the advice not to have children, but as the next lines show, Democritus seems to be fine with the idea of reproduction, if only the risks can be controlled by using other people's children. This is a slightly strange idea, but as we shall see, Plato, in his *Republic*, seems to have addressed exactly that issue. And then, in another fragment, we can detect a more direct threat to the pronatalist hegemony:

> Men think that, by nature and some ancient constitution, it is a matter of necessity to get children. This is plain from the other animals too; for they all naturally get offspring, not with any benefit in view – rather, when they are born, they suffer and rear each as best they can, and fear for them as long as they are small, and grieve if they are hurt. Such is the nature of all things which have a soul; but for men it has come to be thought that some gain actually comes from the offspring.[19]

To interpret this in line with our hypothesis, tradition has it that people should have children for a higher reason, although it is clear that there is none and that, just like other animals, they are following nature's call and then assigning meaning as an afterthought. Plato's response shows how our interpretation may not be as outlandish as it seems.

1.2 First Reaction: Giving Birth to Western Philosophy

A. N. Whitehead, a renowned British logician of the early twentieth century, has been reported to opine: "The safest general characterization of the European philosophical tradition is that it consists of a series of footnotes to Plato."[20] Insofar as he was correct, we can add that in this case Western philosophy can also be seen as a series of responses to outbursts of antinatalist and related thinking.

Plato's *Republic* is a Socratic dialogue that sketches the main principles of an ideal city state, the *polis*, and justifies obedience to its rules.[21] Like his predecessors, Socrates was influenced by Zoroastrian thinking and its tenets.[22] Those were that truth is preferable to tradition; that good and evil form a dualism; and that in an afterlife moral people will be rewarded while the immoral will be punished. The Socrates of Plato's dialogues emphasizes the first of these, the primacy of truth, while Plato himself employs the others in the form of myths when he has a crucial point to make.

In Plato's ideal state, all citizens, according to their ability and inclination, have their assigned classes – they are workers, soldiers, or guardians, all with their designated duties and privileges. The population size is limited, as he specifies in his last dialogue, *Laws*, to 5,040 (= 1 x 2 x 3 x 4 x 5 x 6 x 7) – although slaves, at least, are not included in this count. Reproduction is strictly controlled, expert officials encouraging, behind the scenes, unions between the best individuals to guarantee the best brood. Children are educated by the *polis* and they do not know who their parents and siblings are. Women and men alike can rise to the highest positions. The state is defined by selective eugenic pronatalism with traces of pragmatic gender equality.[23]

The arrangement offers a practical solution to Democritus' first problem, the danger of having one's own unpredictable offspring. Matchmakers secure the quality of future citizens and parents need not look after their children. Democritus' second challenge, the lack of meaning in an atomistic world, was a tougher nut for Plato to crack, and had to be dealt with theoretically, by resorting to myths – accounts that, in ancient Greece, provided a probable explanation for phenomena that could not be fully understood in terms of reason and observation.

According to one such account in Plato's dialogue *Timaeus*, the world was made by a demiurge, an artisan god, who had to produce order and proportion out of the elements available, constrained by the principle of necessity. One interpretation has it that after all the perfect material had gone to constructing the stars, people had to be created out of inferior stuff and were left initially imperfect. Our lives on Earth are needed to reach perfection and to complete the demiurge's work. This explains why we are here and gives our this-worldly existence its meaning.[24]

The ideal state is the setting in which we can fulfill our destinies. By conducting ourselves according to the laws of the republic, we ascertain that creation reaches its goal. In addition, we ourselves stand to gain from the required obedience, because after death our lawful behavior will be rewarded and unlawful behavior punished, as described in the myth of Er in the concluding chapter of the *Republic*.[25]

What can we learn from this? Can we close the case, observe that Democritus was wrong, and note that the good pronatalist order has been restored? Or should we reject Plato's unscientific use of myths and deny that he has proven anything? Luckily, we do not have to go to either extreme. We can identify this sequence of conflicting ideas as the first confrontation between Western philosophy as exemplified by Plato, safeguarding natalism, and – to use Ramesh Mishra's term – rejectionist philosophy as illustrated by the fragments of Democritus and others, questioning meaning and leading the way toward more pronounced antinatalism.[26] The pattern that emerges here has been repeated throughout the history of Western thinking.

The details of Plato's theory were immediately questioned by his contemporaries and followers. Aristotle thought that not knowing one's parents and siblings would be unnatural and lead to incest and loss of healthy family ties. Based on his own philosophy, he suggested more traditional policies both for reproduction and division of labor in the state. Where Plato had relied on myths, Aristotle claimed to build his model on biological and psychological facts. Human beings need nutrition and shelter like all animals; they propagate and raise their offspring; and display a tendency to seek pleasure and avoid pain. In addition to these, our practical reason tells us how we can best reach our goals. A virtuous life without excesses – keeping to the Golden Mean – in a well-ordered society is a reward in itself and gives our lives meaning.[27]

Similarly, Epicurus and Zeno of Citium crafted their own theories, one on the atomism of Democritus, promoting moderation; the other on Socratic teachings as interpreted by the Cynics, stressing the control of one's mind. The preserved fragments of their works have little to say about reproduction but by making life's purpose a more personal matter they did pave the way to the next alarm, which strongly features the philosophical schools they founded, Epicureanism and Stoicism.[28]

1.3 Second Alarm: Virtue and Christianity

Epicureanism, popular in the Greco-Roman world for centuries, was by far the best candidate for carrying the torch of Greek pessimism forward, past Plato's mythical utopia. In the world of atoms, there are no gods or an afterlife to be feared, no greater purpose, and people are free to seek their own happiness in the light of their own reason. It turned out, however, that the message was not acceptable to all. Thinking people were divided into ardent advocates and equally ardent critics, and the picture painted by the opponents was quite unattractive. They saw Epicureans as ungodly, weak gluttons for the most vulgar pleasures and derided the school accordingly. The popular poems of the Roman philosopher Lucretius still kept the doctrine afloat during the first centuries BCE and CE,[29] but the rise of Christianity sank it during the second century CE.[30]

Attitudes concerning the value of life, however, remained ambivalent among other popular philosophies. Cicero, one of the foremost Roman statesmen and a cautious Stoic, was keeping the Wisdom of Silenus well alive when he wrote circa 45 BCE: "[N]ot being born and hence hurled against life's rocks is clearly the best option. Second best, if you do get born, is to die and flee the violence of Fortune as fast as you'd run from a burning building."[31]

While the context of this possibly authentic fragment is not fully known – Cicero consistently taught that having children is a citizen's duty – Seneca, a more pronounced Stoic, also expressed a similar sentiment about life and birth 100 years later:

> Nothing is so deceptive, nothing is so treacherous as human life; by Hercules, were it not given to men before they could form an opinion, no one would take it. Not to be born, therefore, is the happiest lot of all and the nearest thing to this, I imagine, is that we should soon finish our strife here and be restored again to our former rest.[32]

The Stoic philosophy, more in keeping with Roman civic virtue than the relative Epicurean withdrawal, was otherwise in no way death-seeking, but these quotations show that the pessimist idea of life having little redeeming meaning was still around. The Seneca quote is also one of the earliest sources to conceptualize birth as a choice that would not be consented to by as-yet-not-existing individuals – who or whatever they might be.

Also, at this point in history, the Cynics raise their heads. They are highlighted only now because the authorship of texts credited to Diogenes, the founder of the school, is uncertain. This is how his first-century followers saw his teaching:

> One should not wed nor raise children, since our race is weak and marriage and children burden human weakness with troubles. . . .

> But life will become devoid of people. For from where, you will ask, will the succession of children come? I only wish that dullness would leave our life, and that everyone would become wise! For now, perhaps only the one persuaded by me will go childless, while the world, unconvinced, will beget children. But even if the human race should fail, would it not be fitting to lament this as much as one would if the procreation of flies and wasps should fail? For this is what people say who have not observed the true nature of things.[33]

Now, whoever in the first century CE wrote this and for whatever reason, we have here not only a fully fledged expression of antinatalism, and extinctionist antinatalism to boot, but also a confirmation of the sentiment that thinking people who observe "the true nature of things" will see the futility of human life and the reproductive activities that perpetuate it.

In the meantime, Christianity, at first only one Jewish sect among many others, spread and started to exert influence. It needed three centuries to become the official religion of the Roman Empire, but its impact was felt much earlier thanks to the close cultural ties between the Mediterranean realms. Théophile de Giraud gives a good description of the details of Christian antinatalism;[34] for our narrative, two interrelated ideas and their practical execution are pivotal. These are the second coming and the strict virtue of chastity.

Some early Christians counted on Jesus returning soon, maybe during the lifetime of the generation who had witnessed his teaching and works. Since the end times, according to the Gospels, could be quite apocalyptic, it would be dangerous to women to start new pregnancies and give birth to babies. Matthew the Apostle has Jesus describing the events before his return as follows:

> Then you will be handed over to be persecuted and put to death, and you will be hated by all nations because of me. At that time many will turn away from the faith and will betray and hate each other, and many false prophets will appear and deceive many people. ... So when you see standing in the holy place "the abomination that causes desolation," ... then let those who are in Judea flee to the mountains. Let no one on the housetop go down to take anything out of the house. Let no one in the field go back to get their cloak. How dreadful it will be in those days for pregnant women and nursing mothers![35]

Matthew's Jesus then goes on to warn that no one will know the exact time of his second coming before the end-of-this-world calamities are already upon the believers. Women making decisions in the light of this information could well have thought that reproduction would not only be futile but downright perilous for them and, of course, for their children. Both prudence and kindness would have pointed to an antinatalist solution.

Interestingly, the reasons first-century Christians could have held against reproduction are very similar to those women cite today when they are concerned about the environment. Impending ecological disasters threaten the life quality of future individuals and their mothers – and the threat may prompt women to consider not having children.[36] Does this mean that modern antinatalism was born in ancient Rome, just to lie dormant until our day? Of course not. The correct interpretation is that people in the Western world have lived in the shadow of the same imagery for 2,000 years and counting. That this imagery may now be cracking at its seams motivates our normative account in Section 3 of the Element. But we are getting way ahead of ourselves.

In the meantime, decades and centuries passed without the awaited return of Jesus, and the message began to develop in different directions. Some continued to believe in the imminent comeback and saw signs of "the abomination that causes desolation" all around. Others went on with their lives thinking that since whatever will happen later is beyond their control, they had better concentrate on living a virtuous Christian life to secure their salvation. Yet others combined the idea of virtue with a body–soul dualism that had been nascent in Plato's philosophy – and before it Zoroastrian thinking – and now reemerged in Gnosticism and related creeds.

Paul the Apostle was apparently thinking about both the end times and the generally vicious nature of sexual activities when he wrote these famous lines in his Letter to the Corinthians:[37] "Now to the unmarried and the widows I say: It is good for them to stay unmarried, as I do. But if they cannot control themselves, they should marry, for it is better to marry than to burn with passion."[38]

The meaning of the passage has been disputed, but one thing is clear. With some possibly related Old Testament verses,[39] it gave early Christian theologians ammunition against reproduction and marriage and for abstinence and chastity. The most common official interpretation of Paul is that he only cautioned against extramarital sex, but there have been more radical readings.

Gnostic sects were plentiful in the Mediterranean world from the first century CE. They held a variety of beliefs from different sources and some of them viewed marriage and reproduction in a favorable light; but others advocated openly antinatalist, later to be banned as heretic, views. The backbone of Gnosticism was a spirit–matter dualism, in which the soul was considered to be good and everything material evil. This tallies with the Zoroastrian and Platonic understanding of the universe, except many Gnostics took the notion further. Some maintained that there are two deities, Sophia, the perfect worldsoul, and the demiurge (as in Plato), the blind and ignorant creator of the material universe, also sometimes known as Ahriman (Zoroastrianism), Satan (Judaism), and Yahweh (the Old Testament God).[40]

The dualism and the duality of deities are open to interpretation, the mildest being the later Christian orthodoxy of the Devil as a fallen angel in constant opposition with God. The Encratites ("self-controlled"), among others, drew more extreme conclusions.[41] Disparaged more than once by Clement of Alexandria, a major church father, according to Hippolytus of Rome they passed "their days inflated with pride," "abstaining from animal food, being water-drinkers and forbidding to marry," and could be "estimated Cynics rather than Christians."[42] So, if Hippolytus is to be trusted, what we have here is a group of vegetarian and temperant antinatalists who are not particularly liked by the powers that be.

Other ascetic readings of Gnosticism shared the Encratites' view that flesh is the root of all evil. When flesh was defined as sex, the thinking among the mainly celibate bachelors sometimes took distinctly misogynic turns. More abstract and subtle divisions were also presented, as evidenced by the Manicheans and the Neoplatonists, who both occupy a double role in our narrative. Initially a part of the second antinatalist alarm, they were revised and combined by Augustine of Hippo to become the official pronatalist doctrine of the Christian church.

1.4 Second Reaction: Philosophizing Christianity

As we have seen, the second antinatalist alarm was focused on denying the value of birth much more clearly than the vague Greek pessimism before it. The search for meaning in life was ever-present, but worries about the end times and the impurity of the flesh actually led scholars and clergymen to advocate abstinence and strict chastity in practice. By the fourth century CE, Gnostics and Manicheans, earlier grudgingly tolerated, were banned from the Christian community and persecuted.[43]

Augustine of Hippo, eventually a bishop and saint of the Roman Catholic church, started his intellectual and spiritual life as a Manichean.[44] The central tenet of the sect – intended by its founder Mani to combine ancient faiths including Zoroastrianism, Buddhism, and Christianity – was a new variety of dualism. The universe consists of good light and evil darkness, and our visible world is a struggle between the two. Light will ultimately win but every human soul is a particle of light thrown into the darkness and trapped by it. Although salvation is possible, bringing new lives into existence is unkind and inadvisable. Add to this that Mani was regarded among his followers as the last great prophet after Zoroaster, Buddha, and Jesus, the condemnation of the – by now quite pronatalist – church was more than understandable.[45]

Incidentally, as remarked by Masahiro Morioka,[46] Buddhism is the odd one out in this company. While it agrees with the others that salvation or nonexistence – *nirvana* – is to be sought, souls that have left this world imperfected need to reincarnate to continue their quest. Antinatalism as universal nonreproduction would leave these souls stranded for good and cannot therefore be recommended. But back to our story.

The next step Augustine took on his intellectual journey was Neoplatonism, a philosophical school commenced during the third century CE. Its founder, Plotinus, taught that evil (or darkness) is not a substance of its own but, instead, mere lack or privation of good (or light). In the beginning, there was only well-structured good; structureless evil is a result of people distancing themselves from it. The remedy is that we abandon our worldly, material ways and turn toward the other-worldly, spiritual goodness represented by One or God, the creator of everything. This is an inner voyage that Plotinus reported to have completed – he had seen the face of God, so to speak.

For Plotinus, ethics and esthetics coincided in that when we seek to see the glory of God, we also seek to fulfill our own destiny. In his *Symposium*, Plato told a story about the levels we must ascend to understand the true nature of beauty. We begin by loving one particular attractive body, we then go on to love all attractive bodies and minds, realizing that the minds or souls are far more beautiful than the bodies, and end up with the revelation that the abstract form or idea of beauty represented by all beautiful bodies and minds is what we have been looking for. Augustine, following Plotinus, claimed to have made the trip and seen the light.

The Manichean suspicions concerning sex and reproduction as forces of the dark never fully left Augustine. Even later, he returned to Paul's Letter to the Romans: "Let us behave decently, as in the daytime, not in carousing and drunkenness, not in sexual immorality and debauchery, not in dissension and jealousy. Rather, clothe yourselves with the Lord Jesus Christ, and do not think about how to gratify the desires of the flesh."[47] Put together with his youthful involvement with Manichaeism, going too deep into areas like this could have spelled trouble – at least to Augustine's ecclesiastical career. It is possible, as observed by Kevin Coyle and supported by John McKeown,[48] that he lived "his entire Catholic life in dread of being branded a crypto-Manichean"[49] – something that would have had dire consequences.[50] In his main works, however, he redeemed himself by concocting a world history that would become Christian orthodoxy for centuries to come.[51]

The principles on which Augustine founded his ethics were a combination of Manichean, Neoplatonic, and Christian credos. The levels of being are God, spirit, and the body, God being the highest and the body the lowest. Those lower down the scale are inferior to the higher ones and subordinate to them. True Christians should turn from bodily considerations to spiritual ones, and their highest goal is a union with God. Anyone with a Christian upbringing could recognize these basic elements of the faith, even today. There are some crucial points in the account, however, that have kept, or should have kept, philosophers and theologians on their toes.

One is the subordination of spirits and bodies to God. This could, of course, be justified by scripture but, philosophically speaking, the usual explanations do not apply. Socrates, Plato, and other ancient as well as more contemporary thinkers have noted that the aspirations of the mind often produce more permanent satisfaction than physical pleasures. This can be used to support the spirit–body divide and body's subordination to its mental or meaning-seeking counterpart. However, God, in Augustine's model, is of the same substance as the human spirit, only in thicker condensation. There is no qualitative difference like there is between spirit and body, only a quantitative one. How should we interpret this? Does it mean that might is right, that the strong are morally allowed to subjugate the weak, a view philosophers had accused their rivals, the Sophists, of promoting? Surely not.

What else could separate the deity from – essentially – itself and cement the proposed position of authority? The most popular line seems to be that the created are subordinate to their creators. Full stop. No explanation, no justification. They just are. Maybe this has to do with our notions of production and ownership. If we build a house out of materials that we have legitimately gathered from common land, we own it. Similarly, God, who made us out of nothing, owns us. But does the analogy work when beings with minds are involved? Not necessarily.

Humankind is currently developing robots and thinking machines with increasing speed. At some point, it is to be expected that some of the machines will be better than us, more intelligent and morally more evolved. We may think that we own them, whatever their properties, and that they should take orders from us, as per the second law of robotics formulated by Isaac Asimov.[52] This is far from self-evident, though, if the artificial life we have created has surpassed us, perhaps without our knowledge or contribution. Mere initial authorship or formal ownership does not inevitably make subordination legitimate. We shall leave the matter for now, but it will return to our story during some further subalarms and in Sections 3.4 and 3.5 on imposing meaning onto our lives as a vindicator of pronatalism.

Another challenge, duly recognized by Augustine, was that only very few people can expect to ascend the scale of being – as he and Plotinus claimed to have done – and see God during their lifetime. The recompense Augustine offered, following Plato and biblical scriptures, was an eternal afterlife in the

City of God. Problems persist, though, as it would stand to reason that only good people can reach this bliss. Otherwise, what would motivate good, God-fearing behavior? If everyone is automatically rewarded, why bother to be moral? In the opposite case, bad people are left out and our sense of justice is satisfied. But, thinking further, a new question then arises: Why did God create the people who will be excluded? We are, after all, talking about an omniscient, omnipotent being who knows everything, including future events, and can accomplish anything at will. Was God, one might wonder, deliberately unkind in creating people who will be shut out and left in the dark?

Augustine's response relied on a peculiar understanding of freedom of the will. God gave humankind free will in the beginning, so at the dawn of time lawful behavior and eternal bliss were a matter of choice, openly available to us. Unfortunately, however, Adam and Eve had sex against God's orders, produced offspring of their own making, and recreated the human nature. Due to this original sin, they and their descendants were banished from the garden, stripped of free will, and became unable to secure their own salvation. Adam and Eve, in other words, committed all their progeny to potential gloom. Only God's grace, according to Augustine, can guarantee us a place in his City.

This solution is rife with issues that theologians and scholars of religion are still trying to settle.[53] To see what is relevant to our story, however, we have to consider what is obscured rather than what is highlighted. Instead of engaging with learned disputes on determinism, free will, or God's attributes, we can point to a crucial detail that is seldom discussed. It is the crime that sentenced humankind to a life of no choice and impending misery. It is not a moral crime by any usual standards. Adam and Eve were not being unkind or intentionally harming others. They just disobeyed an arbitrary order given by the one who had made them – effectively, their father. Thinking people might well consider their behavior understandable and the morality condemning it weird; but somehow Augustine and his followers have managed to ignore this question. Had they paid heed to the parental imposition, they might have realized how reproducers have created God in their own image, not the other way around. But, again, we are getting ahead of ourselves. Let us move on to some later outbreaks of antinatalism and to the ways in which non-Platonic philosophies handled the intellectual challenge.

1.5 The Long Aftermath of the Second Reaction: Evasive Maneuvers

After Augustine, centuries pass before antinatalism properly returns to our radar. The persecution of the Manicheans and other Gnostics made it unwise to flaunt ideas that went against the orthodoxy of the Roman church. Also, invasions and political turmoil kept Europeans busy. Attila the Hun roamed the continent, Rome fell, other realms rose, the Vikings ransacked everything in their path during their voyages, royal families came and went, feudalism thrived, and crusades were launched to stall the emergence of what was to become the Ottoman Empire, yet another threat to Christian Europe. People do not always have the time for the subtleties of Greek pessimism when they have their hands full protecting their lives and livelihoods.

The intermission could justify closing the case of the second antinatalist alarm and the reaction to it. We have, however, two reasons for considering the next fourteen centuries as a prolonged aftermath of the philosophical reaction initiated by Augustine. The first is that the main threats remained the same. Thinking people's pessimism and doubts about the meaning of life were still there. So, beneath the surface, were heretic Christian musings about the virtues of chastity and abstinence. The second reason is that the reactions, by and large, followed the pattern we have already seen during the first response. Plato was shadowed by Aristotle, Epicurus, and Zenon. Similarly, albeit over a longer period of time, Augustine's work was tracked by Aristotelians, Epicureans, Stoics, and their lineages.

On the alarm side, secular pessimism was exemplified by the eleventh-century Syrian philosopher and poet Abu al-'Ala' al-Ma'arri. Syria is not in Europe but al-Ma'arri lived during the Islamic Golden Age, marked by advances in science and the arts, brought to Europe via Spain, which was then a part of the Muslim world.

Al-Ma'arri's point of departure was reason and the conviction that all religions are essentially a cloak that hides the truth from the ignorant masses. As he wrote: "Do not suppose the statements of the prophets to be true; they are all fabrications. Men lived comfortably till they came and spoiled life. The sacred books are only such a set of idle tales as any age could have and indeed did actually produce."[54] This passage conveys two of al-Ma'arri's views: religions are lies and, in addition, specific to a period and location. Atheism and relativism in the same package. In case anyone would like to challenge him, he had this to say about himself and his potential opponents: "The inhabitants of the earth are of two sorts: those with brains, but no religion, and those with religion, but no brains."[55] A sweeping generalization and a touch of arrogance, maybe, but also a concise expression of the belief that critical ideals need thinking people to take root.

The critical ideals held by al-Ma'arri included, apart from atheism and relativism, asceticism, veganism and antinatalism. With regard to asceticism, he tried to live a simple life and even to keep his poetry out of the reach of the paying public, but he was born to a notable family and became rich anyway, so withdrawal from earthly life was easier for him than for most. He was blinded by smallpox at the age of four, though, and felt isolated from the sighted and his community all his life. Veganism was something he assumed later in life, writing eloquently about the needless suffering of nonhuman animals at the hands of humans.

Al-Ma'arri's antinatalism seems to be genuine but it is a blend of more general sympathy toward fellow beings – as in the case of veganism – and bitterness about his own fate. (The latter is also visible in the Old Testament laments of Job and Jeremiah and possibly in the grief of a family loss in the Cicero fragment we quoted in evidence of Stoic attitudes (see footnote 31). On Al-Ma'arri's tombstone, it says, according to his wishes: "This is my father's crime against me, which I myself committed against none."[56]

We do not know whether he would have felt the same if he had not been blinded and – in his own words – isolated. In a philosophical passage, he seems to move seamlessly from his own predicament to a more universal statement about the value of life:

> Whenever I reflect, my reflecting upon what I suffer only rouses me to blame him that begot me. And I gave peace to my children, for they are in the bliss of nonexistence which surpasses all the pleasures of this world. Had they come to life, they would have endured a misery casting them to destruction in trackless wildernesses.[57]

Since he had no reason to assume that his children would have shared his particular destiny, this seems to be saying that nonexistence would indeed be generally preferable. In other quotations collected and presented by Reynold Alleyne Nicholson, al-Ma'arri goes on to fortify the more universal message: "Procreation is a sin, though not called one";[58] "To beget is to increase the sum of evil";[59] "Refrain from procreation, for its consequence is death";[60] "It is better for a people, instead of multiplying, to perish off the face of the earth."[61] If the context does not defy these reflections – and according to Nicholson that does not seem to be the case[62] – like-minded modern antinatalists can justifiably hail al-Ma'arri as the first all-round unconditional advocate of their creed, right to the point of condoning human extinction (or at least the demise of a specific population), our topic in Section 2 of this Element.

While al-Ma'arri represented free-thinking atheism, two early second-millennium South European sects, the Bogomils in the Balkans and the Cathars in Italy and Spain, carried forward the torch of Christian antinatalism.[63] The sects were Manichean and Gnostic and mainly relied on the traditional arguments of their stem creeds. Good and evil are in competition, spirit is good and flesh is evil, having sex and children, as well as eating animals, are sins, and universal chastity is the only way to salvation. A couple of details are worth mentioning, though.

The Cathar diet was pescetarian – they refused to eat anything that is the product of activities of the flesh, that is, reproductive intercourse. This would seem to imply that the opposition was more to sex than to having offspring. If that were so, present-day Cathars could resort to *in vitro* fertilization and artificial wombs that remove the encounters of the flesh from the equation. More probably, however, the ban would stay on. Cathars believed in a version of the Neoplatonic light–darkness dualism and that humans are God-created spirits trapped in the evil world of flesh made either by the Devil (a separate deity) or Lucifer (a fallen angel). Making children is providing fuel to the dark forces.

The spirit–flesh dualism is not, however, without its theological problems. It seems to make humans too God-like – to give them a semidivine status as beings of the same godly substance. We encountered this issue in Augustine's metaphysics; in his thinking it was further intensified by the story of Adam and Eve inadvertently cocreating the current human nature. The theoretical edifice was crumbling down and at least one of the flaws could be traced back to the already chastised Manichaeism.

If advocating Gnostic views in Europe had always been unwise, by the twelfth and thirteenth centuries it had become downright lethal. Cathars – anyone who could be called Cathar, really – had been identified as heretics of the worst kind and they were persecuted and silenced by the Roman Catholic church.[64] Their brand of antinatalism drifted into oblivion with their demise, but their challenge to prevailing orthodoxy had shown the need to update the Augustinian philosophy that had so far kept official Christianity together.

Thomas Aquinas, the supreme thirteenth-century church father, rose to the challenge.[65] He combined scripture, Augustine, and elements of Aristotelianism as it was filtering to Europe from the Islamic world through Muslim Spain. The most popular interpretation of Aristotle at the time had been formulated in the twelfth century by Abū l-Walīd Muḥammad Ibn ʾAḥmad Ibn Rušd, known as Ibn Rushd or by his Latinized name, Averroes.[66] Ibn Rushd was a notable Andalusian Islamic philosopher whose doctrine, Averroism, was gaining ground in the newly established universities across Christendom. The reading, however, was marked by rationalism and atheism, to the dismay of the church authorities.

Putting reason before faith or tradition had entered the saga before – in Zoroaster, Socrates, and more recently al-Maʾarri – but now the threat was so imminent that the church had to commission their sharpest mind to address it.

Aquinas restored order by arguing that, in a full analysis, faith as found in the church's reading of the scriptures and reason as practiced by the best philosophers come to the same conclusions; and that this is true of all important matters concerning life, politics, and good conduct. To prove his point, he conducted painstaking comparative studies into everything that was brewing in the medieval intellectual world and produced a staggering oeuvre, the *Summa Theologica*, that is still keenly studied today.

In terms of our story, the main innovation made by Aquinas was his description of human beings as God-created agents with a God-given, pronatalist purpose. He agreed with Aristotle that our main goals in life are to survive, flourish, procreate, and act in accordance with our practical reason. In addition to these goals, Aquinas added seeking knowledge of God, an aspiration alluded to by Aristotle as a quest for theoretical understanding and affirmed by Augustine in his spiritual ascent to seeing the maker.

And that, in all its simplicity, is the contribution Aquinas made to the debate over pronatalism and antinatalism. Let us focus on the key concepts to clarify the message, which is well alive in current Roman Catholic teaching. We are made by God, and God has given us a *telos*, goal, meaning, and purpose – to live our lives in harmony with our nature as living, feeling, thinking, social beings. An important part of this is procreation. Chastity has its time and its place,[67] but ensuring that humankind lives on and continues its search for God is an integral part of our existence in his service.

By the way, we use the word "procreation" here for the first time in our narrative, and advisedly so. Before Aquinas, it had been questioned whether humans can be cocreators alongside God or whether, in a dualistic world, this would make us his competitors. This cloud has passed, and we can proudly serve God by being his procreative cocreators.

Aquinas was influential, and one-seventh of the current world population abides by the doctrine he forged. Or do they? That authorities and scholars in the Vatican know his teaching and occasionally issue advice based on it is one thing; yet it is quite another to estimate the impact of abstract philosophies on Catholics in real life. Among the latter, rituals, graphic images, and memorable tales probably make a more lasting impression. These, too, were – and are – in ample supply within the Roman Catholic culture.

One of the memorable tales is Dante Alighieri's *Divine Comedy*, an allegorical poem completed around 1321 that introduces a wide-eyed viewer to the conditions in hell, purgatory, and heaven. The order of the proceedings is a reminder of the soul's journey toward God. In the first circle of hell, Limbo, reside those who did not sin but were never baptized:

> For this defect, and for no other guilt,
> we here are lost. In this alone we suffer:
> cut off from hope, we live on in desire.[68]

The doctrinal determination of who belongs to Limbo is still ongoing in Roman Catholic theology,[69] but the mere idea has two important corollaries. Parents are acting wrongly if they do not baptize their children as soon as possible. And, during the period of colonialism that followed, missionaries and generals would also have acted wrongly had they not baptized the Indigenous populations, against their will if necessary.

The Renaissance jells naturally here with medieval times, Aquinas providing inspiration to Dante and Dante to Giovanni Boccaccio, whose *Decameron* – a collection of 100 short stories, credited as Europe's first novel – in turn stimulated other writers.[70] Boccaccio's themes – often extramarital affairs and the stupidity of the clergy – caused him some trouble with the church but he survived unscathed. We mention him only to point out that the extremely negative attitude toward sex among religious philosophers seems to be relaxing a little here, before the backlashes of Protestantism, Puritanism, and witch hunts that drove female healers out of their traditional roles as minders of women's reproductive health. But that was later. And we were supposed to be talking about philosophies.

After Aquinas, explicitly antinatalist talk drifted out of fashion, but reason, the power that he himself had helped to unleash, started gnawing at the foundations of Christian pronatalism. William of Ocham, a fourteenth-century English philosopher, suggested that when we explain how things are in the world we should always keep the explaining factors and agencies to a minimum. As modern sciences began to advance, this sensible requirement proceeded, slowly but surely, to edge God out of the realm of physics. Rationalist philosophers like René Descartes held on to the idea of an almighty, benevolent spirit but the literal, biblical creator was on the wane. There was, however, still a need for divine intervention in the sphere of morality. The development of revised heirs to Epicureanism and Stoicism testify to this.

The Enlightenment brought earthly happiness to the fore as a psychological good that human beings crave and deserve. In the seventeenth century, a group called the Cambridge Platonists almost made it the cornerstone of their philosophy and opened the route to what would become fully secularized utilitarianism – the insistence that only the maximization of pleasure over pain is worth our moral pursuits.[71] In some of its guises, utilitarianism ended up being an ally to contemporary antinatalism. But there was a bump in the road. In the eighteenth century, George Berkeley, the Anglican Bishop of Cloyne in Ireland, did what Western philosophers have done throughout history and turned the quest for pleasure once again on its head, into a model of implicitly obeying God's orders.[72]

Berkeley admitted that seeking pleasure is good but queried the best way of achieving it. Since we do not know with any certainty what distant consequences our actions will have and how these will affect our well-being, we cannot reasonably judge our choices by their impact. God, on the other hand, being omniscient, omnipotent, and completely benevolent, is in a perfect position to know how we can contribute to the maximization of the good of humanity – which is his goal. In view of this, God has given us a set of rules to follow, in the form of religious prohibitions. If we live by them, we shall, after our earthly life, go on to exist in eternal bliss. In addition to this prudential reason for obeying God and the church, we also, according to Berkeley, have a moral obligation to be subordinate to our maker. In reproductive matters, this means limiting sex to marriage for the purpose of procreation. Versions of theological utilitarianism reached peak popularity in the eighteenth century and lingered on, diluting the religious element, until the nineteenth and possibly twentieth centuries.[73]

Meanwhile, in the European continent, rationalism conquered ground and formal sciences flourished. In the early eighteenth century, Gottfried Wilhelm Leibniz, a German mathematician and philosopher, launched an optimist defense of the God of Protestant Christianity. His view rested on the notions of a preestablished harmony and the best of all possible worlds. In the beginning, God set everything in the universe in motion, like a giant clockwork, and, however bad things may sometimes look from our limited point of view, perfect harmony between all existing entities prevails and the world we live in is the best there can be.[74]

Berkeley and Leibniz complete the philosophical reaction to the second antinatalist alarm and present the last original defenses of the conservative views held by their churches, Anglican and Lutheran. Pronatalism does not even need advocacy, it is a given. Their justifications, however, reflect the fact that some of the seeds of the next antinatalist alarm had already been sown.

1.6 Third Alarm and Reaction: Happiness and Freedom versus a Weaker and Kinder Creator

The third challenge against unquestioned pronatalism has been building gradually for at least the last 300 years. Philosophies come and go, but the main work is done by social and political developments and changes in attitudes in the Western world. Secularization, reason triumphing over tradition, and the ideals of liberty, equality, personal self-determination, and the pursuit of happiness as rights have dented the armor of Christian pronatalism. On the other hand, nationalism has demanded that more children be born for the fatherland, and capitalism requires ever-increasing numbers of able-bodied producers and consumers. These, together with Malthusian concerns about population growth, have fueled often eugenic and always selectively pronatalist policies.

From our historical story so far, four main reasons for not having children emerge: sex is evil; the end is nigh; life is misery; and life has no meaning. Let us see what standings these reasons have as arguments for more current antinatalism.

The conviction that sex is evil has persisted in what we now call Puritan or Victorian attitudes and it may have prevented some births all along. It is also visible in many antiabortion views and other conservative expressions of pronatalist misogyny. Notable philosophers linked with antinatalism, including Arthur Schopenhauer and Søren Kierkegaard, have stressed the value of chastity as well. On the whole, however, fear of sex is not one of the most respectable motivations for opposing births in liberal Western thinking.

That the end is nigh has remained on the agenda for two millennia. From the early Christian belief that Jesus will return soon we have graduated to more social and environmental worries. In connection with the Great Horse Manure Crisis of London in 1894, *The Times* calculated that since horse droppings can be carted out of big cities only by horses, thus producing more droppings, "in 50 years, every street in London will be buried under nine feet of manure."[75] More recently, climate change has been in the limelight.[76] The anxiety this produces has two different forms. Genuinely misanthropic antinatalism suggests that humankind should cease to exist to make room for other species. A milder version proposes that the growth of the human population should somehow be kept under control to secure decent living conditions for all within the planetary boundaries. The features of these creeds are studied in more detail in Section 2 of this Element.

That life is misery has been a consistent theme since the beginning of our narrative. Characters in ancient Greek tragedies and Old Testament stories lament the human lot, as do the Romans, the Christians, and an array of other Europeans throughout the centuries. The difficulty in using any of the expressed sentiments as evidence is that their motivations are often personal rather than universal. Complaints about life's unfairness do not necessarily scale up to philanthropic antinatalism – to abstinence based on compassion toward possible future individuals. And even when contemporary defenders of the doctrine make their universal altruism known, the misery they talk about has to be defined. All lives contain hardships but, barring unbearable agony, these can be endured, especially if there is a purpose that legitimizes them. Although our main emphasis in Section 3 will be elsewhere, we shall also systematically examine the arguments from poor life quality once we get there.

We can assume or invent goals that give purpose to our daily endeavors. No one can deny that – and humankind's skill and tendency to do so will, in fact, be an important part of our refutation of pronatalism. That life has no wider, overall meaning is a more abstract intellectual irritation that only thinking people have. It has, however, proven to be an irritation serious enough to warrant a tradition's worth of denials from Western philosophers. As a result, we have, among others, the castles in the air built by Plato, Augustine, Aquinas, Berkeley, and Leibniz. We are completing the demiurge's imperfect work; following God's plan to save humankind; working with the maker to reach our *telos*; securing our eternal bliss by obeying our benevolent creator's orders; or performing our task as cogs in the mechanism set in motion by the supreme being. Taking our lead from Dante, we can also be actors in the divine comedy produced by God to amuse God.

Put like this, the great philosophical theories that support pronatalism sound ludicrous – but they are when interpreted literally. What evidence is there for the existence of demiurges, gods, and afterlives? For a long time, this question was taken seriously and proofs of the existence of God abounded. Still at the turn of the twentieth century, Henry Sidgwick, the famous English utilitarian, cofounded a Society for Psychic Research to investigate life after death. Had there been evidence of it, he could have concluded with confidence that universal altruism is preferable to rational egoism.[77] Many others just separated religion from ethics and constructed secular moral theories to replace the old ones.

The end of the eighteenth century saw the creation of two of the three theories that still dominate normative philosophical ethics in Western Europe. These were the nontheological utilitarianism of Jeremy Bentham in England and the humanity-focused deontological model of Immanuel Kant in Germany. Both can be bent to support either pronatalism or antinatalism with a convenient choice of additional premises. The third main alternative is Aristotelianism, which was revived under the name Neo-Thomism (as in Thomas Aquinas) at the end of the nineteenth century to hold back the flood of secularization. Neo-Thomism is the official philosophy of the Roman Catholic church and distinctly pronatalist.

During the first half of the twentieth century, most European moral philosophies were more interested in the meaning of ethical sentences than in the meaning of life.[78] Existentialism kept the tragedy of the human fate in the frame but did not take unequivocal stands on whether or not more people should be produced. More and more explicit expressions of antinatalist sentiments began to appear from various directions but they did not reach the mainstream in academia.[79]

The hibernation ended in the 1960s when theologians and philosophers became aware of the ethical challenges posed by advances in medicine and the biomedical sciences. Relatively safe and reliable contraception had become available; pregnancies could be terminated without major threats to women; assisted reproduction was becoming available with artificial insemination and *in vitro* fertilization; and the selection of offspring by genetic testing and modifications loomed large. The branch of applied philosophy and clinical practice coined bioethics was born, and expert opinions were divided on the use of all the new technologies.[80] In a – by now familiar – twist of the tale, however, bioethics, first interested in issues around death like abortion, euthanasia, lethal diseases, and the scarcity of medical resources, soon reinvented itself as a celebration of life and pronatalism.

Conservatives, in the name of sanctity and dignity, tried to stop the use of many technologies to ensure that children continued to be produced in the time-honored way.[81] Many made a point of arguing that the lives created need not be the best possible in every sense. Jennifer Jackson, after admitting that precaution, even with the help of technology, is sometimes wise, wrote: "The commitment to act always in the best interests of children-to-be is, however, extravagant. Parents have a duty to give a good standard of care to their children. They are not obliged always to act in their best interests, whatever sense can be attached to that catch-phrase."[82]

Giving voice to similar disbelief in the case of abortion, David Oderberg opined: "It is often said that every child should be a wanted child.... If a child faces the prospect of coming into the world unloved, however, does it follow that he should be killed? Does 'every child a wanted child' entail 'every unwanted child should be killed'? What is the logic behind the entailment?"[83] Reminding that children should, however, only be had within marital arrangements, Roger Scruton added:

> Marriage does not merely protect and nurture children; it is ... a unique form of social and economic co-operation .... For this is the way that children are made – made, that is, as new members of society, who will, in their turn, take on the task of social reproduction. Society has a profound interest in marriage, and changes to that institution may alter not merely relations among the living, but also the expectations of those unborn and the legacy of those who predecease them.[84]

The conservative take is, then – in a manner reminiscent of Berkeley and Leibniz's not-all-powerful God trying to do his best for humankind under duress – that children must be had in order to continue the line but parents should not be under any special scrutiny regarding the quality of life of their offspring. Reproducers are redefining God in their own image.

Liberals, rooting for autonomy and equality, wanted to make new reproductive methods available to everyone. Warnings against thoughtless reproduction had been sounded from the freedom and happiness camps but they did not carry much weight. In 1851, Arthur Schopenhauer had followed Kant's thinking concerning rational respect for humanity and concluded:

> If children were brought into the world by an act of pure reason alone, would the human race continue to exist? Would not a man rather have so much sympathy with the coming generation as to spare it the burden of existence, or at any rate not take it upon himself to impose that burden upon it in cold blood?[85]

In 1859, John Stuart Mill had, in turn, warned against wanton childbearing and suggested caution: "It still remains unrecognised, that to bring a child into existence without a fair prospect of being able, not only to provide food for its body, but instruction and training for its mind, is a moral crime, both against the unfortunate offspring and against society."[86]

The spirit of liberal bioethics, against these warnings, has perhaps best been encapsulated by Julian Savulescu who, in 2001, introduced his *principle of procreative beneficence*: "[C]ouples (or single reproducers) should select the child, of the possible children they could have, who is expected to have the best life, or at least as good a life as the others, based on the relevant, available information."[87] The idea that genetic information should be used to secure the healthiest and happiest offspring has since been criticized as well as defended, but no one has questioned the more basic premise – that children should be had. What is more, if healthy and happy individuals cannot be produced, then unhealthy and unhappy ones will do. That is what the best "of the possible children they could have" means.

Bioethics, then, quickly chose the side of pronatalism. Under the surface, though, explicitly antinatalist ideas were brewing.

2 Antinatalism and Extinction

Philosophical antinatalism, as it is now known in the English-speaking world, at least, began to take shape in discussions on utilitarianism and future generations in the 1960s. Jan Narveson, who was not an antinatalist, defended the idea that minimizing what is bad takes, in certain cases, precedence over maximizing what is good. Reproduction was his prime example. We have a duty to not bring about bad lives but we do not have a duty to bring about good lives.[88] The claim was a topic of intense controversy in the context of population policies, and the discussion reached its climax in Derek Parfit's 1984 book *Reasons and Persons*.[89] In the wake of Parfit's contribution, philosophers are still quarreling about the "non-identity problem" – whether it makes sense to talk about the interests of individuals who do not exist and may never come to exist. In Section 3 of this Element, we make this question redundant by talking about beings who already exist. Here, however, we focus on what the utilitarian – or, more widely, consequentialist – approach achieved and how it brought to the surface a question that still hangs heavily over contemporary antinatalist debates – the question of human and nonhuman extinction.

It is worth noting, at this point, that the authors of this Element are normatively divided over the matter – we have slightly divergent intuitions about artificial life and the accelerated demise of sentient nonhuman animals. Far from being a hindrance to the development of our narrative, this is an asset in that we can cover more angles with conviction. The differences will be made known as they arise; and since our approach, in this section, is conceptual, they will have no effect on our conclusions. Our normative views will be stated in unison in Section 3.

2.1 Good Lives, Bad Lives, and the Possibility of Different Routes

In 1994, Matti Häyry, who was not yet an antinatalist, expressed Narveson's idea in terms of needs, comparing the situations of reproducers who probably could have a child with a good quality of life ("the healthy and happy couple") and reproducers who probably could not ("the genetically defective couple"):

> Non-existent beings who will never come to existence ... do not and will not have needs which could be satisfied or frustrated. Thus the healthy and happy couple do not have an obligation to procreate.... [Beings] who will come to existence as a consequence of our actions will ... have needs which must be accounted for .... Since the genetically defective couple are directly responsible for the existence of their suffering child, they are also directly responsible for the child's suffering. Their decision to procreate would, therefore, be morally wrong.[90]

The need-based axiology emphasizes the missing duty to have children (of any kind) and the obligation not to have children whose lives would be bad – but the question of permissibility partly remains. Are potential reproducers allowed to have children whose lives would be good? The question remained unexamined, mainly because most philosophers thought that the answer is self-evident: of course people are allowed to have children, probably even children with slightly bad lives.[91] Negative utilitarianism, the creed that suffering should always be minimized and prevented, was unpopular for a reason that was clearly stated by J. J. C. Smart (following R. N. Smart[92]): "For example it is possible to argue that a negative utilitarian would have to be in favour of exterminating the human race."[93] Recommending extinction did not fit the standard utilitarian framework of improving the human lot. Häyry retracted to a more positive formulation of the doctrine (which he has tweaked ever since);[94] and Narveson escaped to libertarianism – basically, the view that our duties are limited to not actively violating each other's fundamental rights.[95]

David Benatar, the paragon of modern antinatalism, broke the deadlock in his seminal 1997 article "Why It Is Better Never to Come into Existence" by maintaining that all lives are bad.[96] He also emphasized the gap between producing good and bad lives, now often referred to as "Benatarian axiological asymmetry." Seana Siffrin, not necessarily an antinatalist herself, followed suit in 1999 by observing that to be legitimate, reproduction would require the prior consent of the prospective individual – something that obviously could not be forthcoming.[97] A confirmed extinctionist since 1998, and reproduction critic since 2004,[98] Häyry completed the basic toolkit of anglophone antinatalism by arguing that the mere risk of a bad life, always present if not always markedly high, makes childbearing irrational and immoral.[99]

We shall come back to these normative ideas as our narrative proceeds. For now, the object of our immediate interest is extinction. If no one has children, humankind will eventually cease to exist. Benatar takes this for granted and says that while it can be seen as regrettable, it is the best alternative overall;[100] Shiffrin has not addressed the topic; and Häyry is on record stating that voluntary human extinction would be a desirable development.[101] The affirmative message has been repeated by negative utilitarians, notably Karim Akerma, an undeservedly neglected pioneer of turn-of-the-millennium antinatalism: "There is no natural necessity for the existence of human beings. . . . Shouldn't we be in favour of mankind's relatively humane dying out rather than advocating a continuation of the way of suffering?"[102]

Others who call themselves antinatalists, however, have mitigated the connection, to the point that they sometimes seem to be in denial about the fate of the species if reproduction should stop.

The current state of affairs is probably due to the consequentialist undertone of the discussion. It is in stark contrast to the attitudes expressed throughout the twentieth century by poets, novelists, and philosophers of other schools of thought.[103] The nihilism and pessimism of, just to mention a few, the existentialists Jean-Paul Sartre and Albert Camus in France,[104] fatalist Peter Wessel Zapffe in Norway, and – preceding all these – the pseudonymous Kurnig in Germany were more in line with our leading theme, the meaning of life. In a 1903 contribution, Kurnig aptly combined his view on the lack of a greater purpose, his irritation at people who do not think, and antinatalism:

> I mourn the creatures you bring into the world who could not defend themselves when you created them, who otherwise would have protested out loud against your action. Since it all boils down to suffering and destruction. Our race serves nothing and exists only as a result of those who, like you, do not examine things thoroughly. Life is suffering; to abstain from procreation is philanthropy and duty.[105]

In 1933, Zapffe, in turn, explicitly connected antinatalism and extinctionism: "Know yourselves – be infertile and let the earth be silent after ye."[106] In a later interview, Zapffe made a crucial distinction: "I am not a pessimist. I am a nihilist. Namely, not a pessimist in the sense that I have upsetting apprehensions, but a nihilist in a sense that is not moral."[107] His latter statement separates an awareness of the lack of preordained purpose in our lives from any clinical depression individuals may experience.

In the patriotic frenzy of the times of Kurnig and Zapffe, there was not much hope of their views becoming widely accepted. It is probably no coincidence that modern antinatalism had its opportunity to emerge at the turn of the millennium. This was, after all, a period during which many intellectuals in Europe thought that history had ended with the collapse of the Soviet Union and that peace would last forever.[108] The megatrends of freedom, equality, and the pursuit of happiness underlying their thinking can be expressed in many ways, but consequentialist optimism has been a prime candidate since the 1990s.

Applied to antinatalism and human extinction, consequentialism is a cause of confusion rather than clarification. It opens the door for empirical comparisons between possible actions and practices, and the disputes can go on endlessly, especially if the asymmetry of good and bad is not accepted. One reading of the facts led to the establishment of the Voluntary Human Extinction Movement in 1991,[109] and later to the rise of at least one radical branch of contemporary antinatalism, namely, efilism, in 2011.[110] These place their trust on finding a reliable, preferably peaceful, way out. Others have interpreted matters differently, as evidenced by David Pearce's notion of The Hedonistic Imperative.[111] Pearce suggests that since humankind will never voluntarily euthanize itself, we should put our hope in gene-editing technologies. He thinks they will help us, within this century, to develop a new human constitution that is not vulnerable to suffering. We can live happily ever after, and if the elimination of suffering is all that there is to antinatalism, proponents of the creed should be content.[112]

Pearce has a solid followership on social media, and he is an antinatalist in the sense that he is childless and recommends it to others, as well.[113] As many members of the antinatalist social media community (if the quarreling threads can be called that) seem to abhor the idea of human extinction, or being responsible for it, or being seen to be responsible for it, Pearce may appear to offer a soothing solution. Going to the conceptual roots, however, we are interested in the feasibility of the separation of antinatalism and extinction even when it is admitted that the two are connected. One side of the case is succinctly put by antinatalist activist and vlogger Lawrence Anton:

> Should the extinction of humans be the or a goal of an anti-procreative movement, and if so why? So my view on that is that, I don't think it's necessary to have it as a goal, I think an anti-procreative movement should be what it says on the tin – it's anti-procreation rather than pro-extinction. Even though being anti-procreation will very likely practically lead to extinction, I think there's an important difference between being anti-procreative and pro-extinction.[114]

Let us see what Anton's – terminologically valid – point amounts to in terms of philosophy. On what conditions, and within which normative views, does the distinction hold?

2.2 Against Reproduction: All, Sentient, and Self-Aware

We approach the connection between antinatalism and extinction by a method of interrogation. We present a general antinatalist claim and ask a series of questions about it. The answers produce a classification of forms of antinatalism and indicate the responses to extinction within them. When a variant of the creed has been defended in the literature or on social media, we summarize the defense. When we hit a currently empty box in our periodic table of elements (to use an analogy from chemistry), we formulate the view ourselves in the light of our best understanding. Figure 1 sketches our table.

The general claim is: "I am against reproduction." In some sense, every antinatalist should be able to stand behind this. People who are for reproduction can more aptly be called natalists or pronatalists.

Our first question is: "All or some?" If the answer is "All," we have a follow-up query: "Does this include the creation and autonomous self-replication of entities beyond carbon-based organisms?" By entities beyond organisms we mean, among other things, artificial intelligence (AI), machines, androids, and extraterrestrial (ET) "life" forms with a noncarbon constitution. As far as we know, none of these exists in an autonomously self-replicating form, but virtual realities and humanoid robots have been intensely developed already, and the fact that we do not know of the existence of aliens does not mean they do not exist.[115]

To be against the reproduction of extraterrestrials would, of course, be a markedly exotic stance. There is, however, a new field of applied philosophy called space ethics that could address the issues involved, perhaps under the title

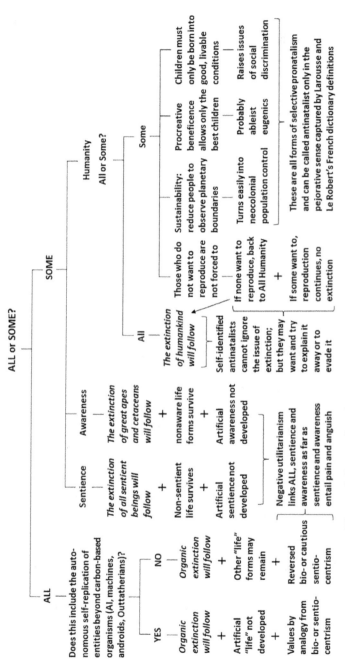

Figure 1 Connections between extinction and being against reproduction.

extraterrestrial antinatalism (ETAN). One issue here is whether someone with this outlook should advocate human reproduction until the aliens arrive and instruct the then living humans to persuade the visitors to stop having offspring? Or would it be enough to leave antinatalist literature lying around for them to find? Would they understand it and would they do as instructed? Or – more intriguingly – will they never come because they have reached the conclusion themselves before trying to contact other species? That would be an answer to the Fermi Paradox – the apparent discrepancy between the probability of intelligent life in the known universe and our lack of evidence regarding its existence. "Where is everybody?," Enrico Fermi famously asked.[116] "Already wisened up and gone?," extraterrestrial antinatalists optimistically answer.

To be against the development of advanced AI is a slightly less unusual position. Thomas Metzinger, for instance, has expressed the concern that human-made thinking machines would probably end up being sentient – capable of suffering in some way that we can grasp if not exactly define.[117] Artificial-intelligence antinatalism (AIAN, or Anti-AI-Natalism as it has been called),[118] could deduce from this that the development should be halted lest we "give birth" to suffering individuals, maybe billions of them through serial production. The analogy with the births of living beings would become tighter with the assumption that the new machines could in time make more machines like themselves.

Champions of AIAN could, however, also reach a completely different conclusion. As Metzinger suggests in a thought experiment, a super-clever and super-compassionate machine could come to understand that humans suffer but are too biased toward existence to escape their condition themselves. The wise and kind device, also in complete control of what goes on in the world, could then painlessly wipe out humankind and perhaps other species, too. There are ethical theories that would see this as desirable – but more on those later.

If nonorganic entities are excluded, the next logical step is to hinder all living Earth dwellers from having offspring.[119] This position could, with a creative interpretation of some existing axiologies, be based on what can be called reversed biocentrism. Biocentrism in its original form states that all life has positive value and should be protected. The reversed version would say that all life has negative value and should be eliminated. This view is known in antinatalist and related discussions as efilism – the ism of "life" spelled backward. The negative value could be intrinsic (life is horrible) or instrumental (life, in and of itself innocuous, can develop into horrible directions). Efilism takes the former stand. In the latter case, the actual value basis could be different – for instance, sentiocentric. Our idea here becomes clearer as we fill in the next two boxes in our schema (Figure 1)

If the answer to the question "Are you against all or some reproduction?" is "Some," then we have several further options. The first is sentience, the ability to feel pain or anguish. In antinatalist debates, sentiocentrism and biocentrism are not always adequately separated. The confusion is partly due to the fact that efilists tend to concentrate on the reduction of suffering although their eventual target is the elimination of all life. For our analysis, the distinction is clear. Being against sentient reproduction means being against sentient reproduction, including that of human and nonhuman animals, extraterrestrials, and machines. Eventually, this entails accepting the extinction (or noncreation) of all these forms of being. Nonsentient entities, including plants and bacteria, may survive, unless they are seen to be a threat. Left behind, they could, in time, once again develop sentience, and the chain of suffering would remain unbroken – not an acceptable result in this conceptual box.

Consciousness, or self-awareness, could be an independent alternative, between purely hedonistic sentience and some more elevated notion of humanity. Apparently, this has not attracted much attention, except insofar as the ability to suffer and the ability to be aware are sometimes likened. This seems to be the case when Benatar, discussing the meaning of life, writes in passing: "Conscious life, although but a blip on the radar of cosmic time, is laden with suffering – suffering that is directed to no end other than its own perpetuation."[120] He does, however, also identify self-awareness as a higher form of consciousness, so the issue may be merely terminological.[121] The motivation of including the concept of self-awareness here is that being aware of oneself as a subject of mental states in the past, present, and future – to use a technical term, being a psychological person – has been a prominent concept in discussions on abortion. Some believe that pregnancies can be terminated at any stage because embryos and fetuses are not persons in this sense. For our investigation, this introduces a new dimension. Maybe existence is undesirable only to beings who are aware of themselves in this way – most human beings, all other great apes, cetaceans, maybe pigs, dogs, and others, not forgetting aliens and artificial beings. In a – once again, reversed – axiological move, it could be argued that the opposition to reproduction should be extended to just these beings, not to all those who happen to live, metabolize, or seek pleasure and shun pain.

2.3 Against Reproduction: Human – All and Some

Moving on, our next port of call is reproduction by humans, all of them and only them. In a standard utilitarian framework, this is a category that can only exist by stipulation – by artificially limiting the scope of morality to members of *Homo sapiens*. As long as utilitarian calculations are based on some measurable experiences, species should make no difference within them. As the founder of secular utilitarianism, Jeremy Bentham wrote about nonhuman animals from his sentiocentric perspective: "The question is not, Can they reason?, nor Can they talk? but, Can they suffer?"[122] In other words, none of the features defining competent, adult human beings – like the ability to reason or talk – are relevant if the focus is on pleasure and pain. And even if they were, reasoning and talking nonhumans should be included.

Bentham's approach, or something resembling it, is visible in the work of most current antinatalist philosophers, at least those who lean toward consequentialism. Benatar is well aware that his arguments against creating new lives apply to nonhuman as well as to human animals;[123] Akerma advocates the sterilization of animals in the wild;[124] and Häyry, while stopping short of wildlife extinction, roots for the end of factory animal production.[125] Antinatalist activists on social media share this mindset and often see veganism as a sibling ideology to their own.[126] Not that it has any bearing on our conceptual analysis, but the activist half of our authorship would, for reasons of efilist consistency, go with Akerma and promote wildlife extinction, as well.[127] These are minor differences in the bigger scheme of things.

The desire to keep anti-procreation and pro-extinction apart, as expressed in the comment by Lawrence Anton cited in Section 2.1, may be linked with suspicions regarding the sentiocentric consensus and especially its theoretical foundation. Negative utilitarianism is a patent solution for opponents of reproduction at any level. Define consciousness or pain or living as bad and the creed will prohibit births. But if everyone abides by the prohibition, something – conscious, sentient, or living beings – will go extinct. And while this could be palatable as an unwanted secondary consequence, negative utilitarianism does not allow this description. If the demise of living, sentient, or conscious beings is the best way to minimize bad, it is our duty. And now that we have reached the human category, it would be our duty to eliminate our own species. That would have happened in all the previous cases, as well, but now the obligation stares at us. Is there any decent way out? We take this to be Anton's question and address it after we have completed filling in Figure 1.

The next step is to confine the advice not to reproduce only to those who are not willing to have children. In this solution, the negative utilitarian duty in its strict form evaporates, leaving only a permission and a strong recommendation to abstain.[128] As long as we hope everyone heeds the advice, however, the question of extinction remains. If no one has children, humankind slides into demise, voluntarily but nonetheless. We could, of course, also hope that only some people cease to reproduce, but then the anti-procreative attitude would be lost. Our remaining three categories share this feature.

Reproduction could be curbed in the name of ecological sustainability – to ensure that the planet remains livable. This would be antinatalist in the sense suggested by the French dictionaries, but since it would allow some births, population control would be an equally good designation. The way population control is implemented in international practice is, of course, open to accusations of colonialism. People in the affluent countries of the Global North are encouraged to multiply while people in poorer countries in the Global South are urged to reduce their offspring. We could call this selective pronatalism on the basis that it quite clearly supports further births, and in a discriminatory manner.

Reproduction could also be curbed on eugenic grounds, as in Julian Savulescu's proposal to have only the genetically best children that reproducers can have.[129] Whether or not specific genetic factors determine the quality of human lives as Savulescu seems to believe and whether or not low-quality lives of this ilk should be particularly avoided are contested issues. Suffice it to say that there are uncertainties and that, in any case, the model is blatantly ableist. For our purposes, the main problem is that this, too, is selective pronatalism, not even intended to reduce birth rates.

Finally, we have a category already identified by John Stuart Mill who in 1859 wrote about the "moral crime" of having children when one cannot "provide food for its body [and] instruction and training for its mind."[130] To be fair, this was more a caution than a prohibition, as Mill conceded that in the worst case the state can step in and fulfill the obligation to children, but it also sows the seeds of a population policy based on social stratum. It would be good if poor people had no children, whereas those who can afford the sustenance and education can continue their reproductive activities. This is another example of selective pronatalism.

As regards the last three categories, our question is, why confuse matters by calling them antinatalism (if anyone is inclined to do so)? We have only included them here because their champions can say, truthfully, that they are against some reproduction, the first theme in Figure 1. As for the second theme, extinction, selective pronatalism shares antinatalism's problem, only on a more confined scale. Third-world populaces, disability groups, and the precariat would be in the line of fire. But now for the central question presented by Anton. Could the shadow of extinction somehow be either explained away or evaded?

2.4 Explaining Extinction Away

We begin by translating the first question – could the shadow of extinction somehow be explained away? – into the language of morality. Are we permitted to cause the extinction of a defined group, say, humankind, in our otherwise laudable attempt to reduce births? If we are, the issue has been explained away. Three responses stand out.

According to the Neo-Thomist doctrine of double effect,[131] an act that has two outcomes, a good one and a bad one, is permissible if and only if four conditions are met:

(i) The act is in and of itself morally good or at least neutral.
(ii) The bad outcome is not directly willed or intended.
(iii) The good outcome is not a consequence of the bad outcome.
(iv) The good outcome is proportionate to the bad outcome.

An example of a morally permissible act would be rescuing people from a burning house even at the cost of breaking arms and legs in the process. This is because (i) rescuing people is good; (ii) the rescuer would avoid doing any damage if that were possible; (iii) the broken limbs do not cause the survival of the rescued; and (iv) saving lives at the cost of inflicting reparable harm is proportionate. Could the doctrine be applied to the case of antinatalism and extinction as well?

The first condition is easily met. Being against – let us say, conservatively, all human – reproduction should be seen as morally good or neutral by antinatalists of any kind.

The second is trickier. Would antinatalists who oppose reproduction avoid causing human extinction if they could? The answer depends on the reasons they have for their view. If they object to childbearing, say, because giving birth harms women, they could evade humankind's demise by investing in artificial wombs. But most modern antinatalists seem to be motivated by the badness of future lives. Insofar as they are so motivated, avoiding extinction does not appear to be a logical solution.

The third condition is useful in that it makes the anti-procreation–pro-extinction divide understandable. One of the doctrine's standard applications in medical end-of-life decisions is to draw a moral difference between euthanasia and pain relief. Even if physicians know that increasing medication will hasten their patient's death, they are, according to the doctrine, allowed to do so. They remove suffering (good outcome) and this (or, to be more precise, its agent) causes death (bad outcome). They are not, however, allowed to purposely hasten their patient's death to remove suffering. This would make the bad outcome the cause of the good outcome, which is forbidden.

Utilitarians find the use of such mental reservations a form of self-deception, but the doctrine of double effect explains one prominent phenomenon in the antinatalist discussion. Some activist vloggers are attracted to a thought experiment that goes by the name The Big Red Button. It consists of a question: "You have a button in front of you. If you press it, the entire world will disappear. Do you do it?" Many philosophers, to the activist vloggers' disappointment, refuse to give a direct yes-or-no answer and explain, instead, that a straightforward negative utilitarian probably would and others probably would not. In our present context, the difference might be the same as the one between anti-procreation and pro-extinction in Anton's plea. The thought experiment offers, so to speak, antinatalism by extinction. When the button has been pressed, there are no more births. Although the end result is the same, Anton and his fellow thinkers prefer extinction by antinatalism.

The fourth condition could present a challenge. That the outcomes are proportionate means that a significant good is achieved while a relatively insignificant bad is allowed. In the euthanasia case the bad, death, may seem significant but the point there is that the patient is fading away already and the remaining life would not offer much. Philosophers and activists who call themselves antinatalists are, however, divided over the worth of humankind's continued existence. Efilists assign it a negative value while others seem to hesitate. Those who hesitate do not have a particularly good case for employing the doctrine of double effect.

Our summary analysis of the doctrine of double effect does not support antinatalism's moral rightness or give definite answers to the underlying conceptual questions but it does throw light on some disagreements within the community. Diverse theories and intuitions lead to diverse views and priorities, and that is understandable. Let us add two more variations to the allowing-extinction-reluctantly box before we go on to views that try to evade the demise.

Extending our investigation to nonconsequentialist views, Julio Cabrera has proposed a deontological defense of anthropocentric antinatalism. Cabrera's starting point is Immanuel Kant's influential humanity principle: "Act in such a way that you treat humanity, whether in your own person or in the person of any other, never merely as a means, but always at the same time as an end."[132] Cabrera's own theory is much more complex, based on his logic and ethics of negativity,[133] but for our present purpose he can be interpreted as arguing that people treat their children as mere means by bringing them into an existence that is inevitably manipulated and controlled by the parents. Since this is a violation of the humanity principle, we have a categorical duty not to have children, with the implication that Cabrera need not necessarily take extinction – as a "second effect" – into account at all. In Kant's well-known example, we are not allowed to tell a lie even if truth-telling would gravely harm others. The harm is regrettable but we are not to blame for it. Similarly, abstinence could be our duty regardless of the consequences. The species may go extinct and that may be unfortunate but it is not our fault. This would, in addition to the doctrine of double effect, be a way of swiping the question of extinction under the carpet.

The Kantian solution, if feasible, would, like unrevised negative utilitarianism, confirm that we can have a moral duty to bring about the demise of humankind. Another way forward would be to revise consequentialism by adding to its requirements a side constraint of autonomy.[134] This fits the box marked "Those who do not want to reproduce not forced" in Figure 1. While it is, as such, no more than a call for reproductive autonomy, the recognition of people's (and maybe other animals') drive to govern and direct themselves can lead to extinction. If no one wants to reproduce, the outcome is inevitable. The trick here is that causing the outcome to materialize is not a moral duty anymore. The philosopher half of the authorship believes in this solution, whereas the activist half does not. Both accept voluntary human extinction but the activist argues, on efilist and purely sentiocentric negative utilitarian grounds, that the proposal does not adequately address the suffering of nonhumans in the wild. We agree to disagree and continue our efforts to find a better formulation. Since our normative account in Section 3 concentrates primarily on humans, the difference does not hinder our efforts there.

2.5 Postponing and Evading Extinction

The philosophical explanations establish that extinction does not have to be an explicit aim in antinatalism. They do not, however, remove the possibility that, left free to choose, all people could refuse to have children and thereby cause humankind's demise. That even this route to voluntary human extinction scares pronatalists is clearly expressed in Richard Ashcroft's description of the shift in Matti Häyry's thinking from 1994 through 1999 to 2004:

> While in 1999 there is an ambiguous note to his suggestion that voluntary extinction be "condoned," ... by 2004 the ambiguity has passed and Häyry is advocating quite explicitly a voluntarily extinctionist position. ... In retrospect, his admirably liberal and humane, dare I say Enlightenment, version of utilitarianism of 1994 has now been fully driven out by a Schopenhauerian version of utilitarianism, in which the only reason not to annihilate the human race (and other sentient creatures) is that doing so coercively would create even more anguish, through the violation of autonomy and the frustration of certain basic, if irrational, needs.[135]

Ashcroft goes on to explicate why Häyry's later view is mistaken, but the disbelief of the passage speaks for itself. Humankind must continue its existence. Our quest in this concluding subsection of Section 2 is to find out how this sentiment can be made compatible with antinatalism. The main options are transhumanism, posthumanism, and ahumanism.

The most popular transhumanist idea within the antinatalist community is David Pearce's suggestion concerning "The Hedonistic Imperative." By making good use of biotechnology, Pearce argues, future people could become radically less prone to suffering and anguish – evolutionary hangovers, needed in the past but not now – and much more prone to pleasure and happiness. Not just any happiness, either:

> So humanity's future ... is not ... an eternity spent enraptured on elixirs of super-soma or tanked up on high-octane pleasure-machines. Nor is it plausible that posterity will enjoy only the dullish, opiated sensibility of the heroin addict. Instead, an extraordinarily fertile range of purposeful and productive activities will most likely be pursued. Better still, our descendants, and in principle perhaps even our elderly selves, will have the chance to enjoy modes of experience we primitives cruelly lack. For on offer are sights more majestically beautiful, music more deeply soul-stirring, sex more exquisitely erotic, mystical epiphanies more awe-inspiring, and love more profoundly intense than anything we can now properly comprehend.[136]

First published in 1995, Pearce's manifesto is a – dare we say hilarious – remnant from a time of unlimited technological optimism in the recent past. The fact that new generations are drawn to his message is perhaps best understood as a kind of historical myopia. "The Hedonistic Imperative" is a typical example of the solutions that capitalism offers to problems that should be handled morally, socially, and politically. If the environment is degrading due to overproduction and overconsumption, capitalism's response is to develop new gizmos that will allow us to produce and consume more.[137] Pearce's promise, far from being kept three decades on, does the same, indirectly encouraging reproduction.

The connection to our topic is that Pearce calls himself a soft antinatalist. This, apparently, means, to him, a combination of personal childlessness and a commitment to negative utilitarianism. It is good to reduce and to prevent suffering; and not having offspring is one way of achieving that goal. Pearce does not, however, believe that humankind would voluntarily go extinct – this, he thinks, is a sociological impossibility. Abiding by "The Hedonistic Imperative," on the other hand, is in his view only a technological challenge and therefore the best alternative available to us. Whatever the merits of his comparison, Pearce provides a get-out-of-jail-free card for those who want to reduce suffering, deny extinction, and possibly also have children. Proposing soft antinatalism and enabling pronatalism like this may appeal to some but has a loud schizophrenic ring to it.

Another transhumanist way to evade the demise of humanity would be immortality. Lawrence Anton, still on the case of keeping antinatalism and extinction distinct, is on record as saying:

> Let's say someone comes up with some sort of serum where they can give the highest bidder immortality. They won't die unless they're killed by someone else, but they aren't going to die of old age. I would have no issue with people taking that or handing it around as long as it's not being forced on anyone and people are sensible about it and have a way to opt out afterwards if they so choose to. I've got no issue with that, whereas I would say that probably conflicts with a pro-extinction view because you're intentionally keeping around the species longer. Whereas I don't think it conflicts with an anti-procreative view because as long as those people don't procreate then it's not pro-procreative.[138]

Anton's idea stems from the same golden era of technological optimism as Pearce's. Liberal bioethicists, notably John Harris, were hot on the topic of immortality in the 1990s and defended it against anyone who had any doubts.[139] The requirement of not having children was a counter-counterargument. If people keep living forever and reproducing at the current rate, the world will be overpopulated on an unforeseen scale, the opponents said. But we can make it a prerequisite that immortals are not allowed to breed, responded Harris.[140]

Insofar as Anton means to make only a conceptual point, he is correct. It is possible to be against births and opposed to extinction at the same time: abstain, yet hope that the immortality treatments will be developed in time to rescue humankind. We do not wish to comment on the probability of the advances involved but we do want to note that, as sensibly worded by Anton, the technology in its envisaged forms postpones rather than prevents the extinction of the species.[141] Biomedical solutions may slow down or hinder aging, but people will still die through accidents and violence. Eventually, someone will have to switch off the light if new people are not born.

A more recent, posthumanist way to avoid extinction yet remain childless could be offered by virtual reality. We are already connected to all manner of smart gadgets and new ones enter the market every day. If this trend continues, we could, sooner or later, depart our biological existence altogether and become voluntary parts of a virtual world, or so some like to think.

Science enthusiasts talk about mind uploading lightly, perhaps thinking of a game world that we could immerse ourselves in temporarily. The real thing would most probably be different from anything that we can currently comprehend. We have no scientific understanding of what it would be or feel like. But this may be looking in the wrong direction. Perhaps the lackadaisical approach stems from our more deeply rooted unscientific, possibly religious or philosophical, beliefs.

Bodily resurrection is a doctrine so familiar to many of us that it does not raise any eyebrows, although it arguably should. When our bodies die, our souls remain alive, maybe asleep, maybe in purgatory, until the two are joined again to live eternally and blissfully in heaven. Science enthusiasts may see mind uploading as an analogous process. We leave our material bodies, get organized into digital, immaterial form, and then enter computer paradise and live happily ever after.

Rebirth presents a similar analogy. The soul of a living being survives biological death and migrates into a new body of the same or another species. This allows the life to be quite different from the original, as in the case of mind uploading. Whether we can genuinely understand what it would mean to be reborn as a bat is another matter. And rebirth is, for good reason, we believe, depicted as a curse rather than a blessing. It could, in fact, be a warning against the dream of virtual existence.

Philosophically speaking, as we have seen in Section 1 of this Element, the primacy of the immaterial aspect of our being is a recurring theme in the European tradition, at least since Plato. According to him, only souls can live in the superior reality of perfect ideas. Augustine of Hippo and Thomas Aquinas echoed the idea in Christian teaching. René Descartes' semisecularization of the soul perpetuated the mind–body dualism that is still tangible in many forms of Western thinking; and after Descartes, subjective idealists like George Berkeley dropped the body out altogether.

From the antinatalist viewpoint, the question is, would mind uploading preserve personal identity or would it create a new individual? Due to the uncertainty of what the end product would be, we might have reasonable grounds to think that the emerging entity would be a novel, different human or posthuman being. The material foundation would be different and there would be a marked discontinuity in the immaterial dimension as well. Mind uploading would, then, kill us and give birth to a life of its own, resembling us in some respects but not identical to us. It would not necessarily be the model of immortality-without-procreation that could support nonextinctionist antinatalism.

Yet another form of antinatalism that does not reject the continuity of life is outlined by ahumanism, or abolitionist vitalism, strongly linked with the emerging discipline of queer death studies.[142] Patricia MacCormack, the main representative of the view, writes:

> There is no meaning to our lives, there is nothing eternal in our deaths, but this does not preclude us from making the lives we lead ones that care for the world and care for the connections, distant and near, acknowledged and secret, that allow the potentia of nonhumans and environments to proliferate by our becoming host in our absence and by our leftovers.[143]

We understand MacCormack to state that all species are equal and that humankind must shrink away to accommodate the needs of all. *Homo sapiens*, as the species it now is, will disappear and a new, more harmonious kinship between nonhuman animals and environments will emerge. People as such do not exist anymore; yet their lives go on through the caring practices they were involved in while they were still around, in a world where hegemonies are abolished and a novel vitality flourishes.

This view, in all its slightly new-age gloss, at least in the eyes of the untrained, is both antinatalist and extinctionist in important ways. It takes the French dictionary definitions to their limits by reducing purely human birth rates to zero. And it prophesizes the demise of *Homo sapiens* as we know it. It does not, like sentiocentric negative utilitarianism, take the extra step of promoting the elimination of other life forms, but then, as a form of vitalism, or biocentrism, it would not. Like the human bioimmortality and virtual human continuity approaches, ahumanism does have a science fiction quality, but considering the topic here, human extinction, that is perhaps to be expected. All in all, it is a feasible narrative for those who believe that, in the absence of people, the lion can lie down with the lamb.

2.6 A Note on Sources and Moving On

A note on our sources in this section is in order. We have used – in addition to philosophical texts – manifesto passages, church teachings, academics' personal opinions, and excerpts from an activist's musings. This has been a deliberate choice. The question of antinatalism and extinction is approached within the community in terms of this kind of material more than technical philosophy and peer-reviewed research contributions.

Having said that, the conceptual message that we are trying to convey shines through. As we have seen, there is more to philosophical antinatalism than utilitarianism, let alone negative utilitarianism, although the latter occasionally tries to monopolize the field. At the same time, we have seen that the demise of humankind, made visible by these views, is something to be reckoned with by anyone opposing reproduction. An escape to the explanations we have given – the doctrine of double effect, Kantian categorical duties, and autonomy-respecting consequentialism – is possible; and so is an evasion relying on transhumanism, posthumanism, or ahumanism. But that extinction has to be addressed in one way or another by any account of antinatalism has now been established. This was needed for our narrative; now we are ready to proceed to our normative account, to preempt, internally, the criticism that if everyone accepts our view, humankind will cease to exist.

3 Procreative Self-Corruption

We have now proceeded to the normative part of our endeavor. Since we do not claim that everyone thinks or should think exactly like we do, let us begin by presenting our shared beliefs. Antinatalism for us means – among other things – that we do not have children, we do not intend to have children, and we would be pleased if everyone acted like us in this respect. By "we would be pleased" we recognize the requirement of consistency in moral matters. We do, and teach, only what we *can* and *do* want others to do and teach. In return, we expect our pronatalist opponents to respect the same general principle. It is not a controversial one. All ideologies that embrace the fundamental equality of moral agents hold the same demand in some form – Christians in the golden rule,[144] consequentialist moralists in the expectation of impartiality,[145] deontological ethicists in the categorical imperative,[146] and so on.

To demonstrate why we are antinatalists, and why we would be pleased to see everyone joining us, we present, in what follows, the standard defenses of contemporary Western antinatalism; our own core views on what is wrong and what is right; a revised risk argument against reproduction; and potential objections to it. These bring us back full circle to the meaning sought by the ancient Greeks; we conclude the Element (Section 3.6) by highlighting the differences between finding purpose via pronatalist and antinatalist routes.

3.1 The Standard Arguments for and against Having Children

Since antinatalism stands in direct opposition to pronatalism, it is useful to begin with the sentiments among those who wish to perpetuate reproduction. These are not always explicitly articulated, as childbearing is the unquestioned default value in Western societies, but we can gain insight from critical reactions to antinatalism. As in Section 2 – where we used Lawrence Anton's position as a springboard – we have chosen one voice to represent the pronatalist temperament. Corey Anton, a passionate defender of reproduction,[147] provides us with an excellent starting point in these selected discussion extracts:

> None of us choose to come into existence, another person makes the choice. They make that choice because their sense is that their life has been more good than bad. ... It's the responsibility of trying to give another person experiences that they have cherished so much ... and they think that they are conferring a benefit on someone who couldn't speak on their own behalf.[148]
>
> When you take a person that's had a lot of suffering, athletes as an example, and they say, "I'm willing to endure this suffering, so don't you be worried about wanting to end the suffering for me, because I want the suffering as a source of transcendence, and a source of growth." You don't get the right to deny them that

pain, you keep calling pain a bad thing, you use it as a justification to deny them life, and the truth is if they want that pain, you're imposing on them.[149]

The person who makes the decision – the person who says, "I need to abort," they may likely go, "My life has sucked, it's been hardship, I'm not going to impose that on another person." Somebody else, they go, "Oh my word, I am about to share with a person the greatest thing that there is, which is knowing that this is [*sic*]."[150]

So if a person believes that sentience and life begins at conception, then here the issue of rights comes it. This is a person that has rights, and it's their right not to be imposed upon. And yet the irony is that there's no way not to make an imposition. It would seem, as best I understand it, it would seem that it's just as much an imposition to tell this person, now that you're conceived, you have to enter life, as it would be to impose upon them your belief that life is an imposition. That is their right . . . to decide for themselves whether or not it is an imposition first, and then second, whether or not the imposition of life is a warrant for a non-entrance into life.[151]

The message that we hear in these quotes can be summed up in four partly overlapping credos and pleas: "Life is good, forward the gift!," "Give life a chance, even with the pain involved!," "Life's wonderfulness makes up for any hardship!," "Let them decide for themselves!"[152] We do not mean to oversimplify the pronatalist case but these soundbites set the scene for the standard defenses of antinatalism: lack of consent, manipulation, the poor quality of human lives, and risk.

As an aside for now (though a theme that we will return to as our story unfolds), those who want to give a chance to nonhuman as well as human lives can choose a more misanthropic tack. Patricia MacCormack is a prime example, advocating a human extinction that would make room for other species.[153] But more on that later.

It should be noted that we do not intend our short descriptions to offer full analyses of the views. Nor are the counterarguments or counter-counterarguments meant to yield decisive normative conclusions. We accept all defenses of antinatalism and are, for now, only building toward our own view.

Seana Shiffrin addressed the "Let them decide for themselves!" plea directly by arguing that consent would indeed be required for reproductive choices. Unfortunately, however, those who do not exist yet cannot give it – as they do not yet exist. According to Shiffrin, we cannot proceed by assuming their permission, either. Assumed consent is a possibility only when harms are prevented, not when supposed benefits are conferred.[154] Anton recognizes the conundrum but dismisses it by marveling what a "miraculous occurrence" life is.[155]

Julio Cabrera had already, before Shiffrin, drawn attention to the one-sidedness of reproductive decision-making. His double-barreled argument has it that, first, to bring a new life into existence is unilateral manipulation by the parents;[156] and second, that when the child is born, the manipulation continues. The new individual is burdened, to use a recent phrasing by Cabrera, by the "risk of procreation," "the risk of manipulating and harming others," and "the risk of not being able to end one's own life with dignity."[157] Such pessimism concerning life's moral wickedness fails to resonate with Anton's optimism but our own view will reflect Cabrera's concerns.

Shiffrin and Cabrera's focus is on the intrinsic legal or moral wrongness of parental choices. A more popular approach has been to appeal to the suffering of future individuals. The intensity and nature of the envisioned suffering varies from one interpretation to the other.

The pseudonymous efilist Inmendham paints the gloomiest picture in his innumerable contributions on social media. We have been violated to exist and Anton's war cry "Give life a chance!" is an invitation to repeat similar violations in the hope that the next person will like it.[158] The efilist rhetoric has been fiercely debated within the antinatalist community,[159] and the heated exchanges between Inmendham and Anton are well documented.[160] One thing stands out, though. If the efilist view on life's utter horribleness is accepted, all forms of reproduction – including nonhuman reproduction – should be rejected forthwith.

David Benatar's description of the misery of existence is expressed in polite academic terms but it is equally radical. He is on record as saying that "even the best lives are very bad."[161] For him, then, statements like "Life is good," "Life is wonderful," and "Life is a gift" are simply untrue. Life is a burden that should not be bestowed on new individuals. Benatar also preempts the pronatalist case for any obligation to have children for their own sake. The asymmetry between not bringing about bad (a duty) and bringing about good (not a duty) in reproduction removes this possibility even if they could have a decent quality of life. Anton, due to his hopeful premises, disagrees.

Matti Häyry, recognizing that people do not generally acknowledge Inmendham and Benatar's grim take on life's value, has formulated a considerably thinner version of hedonistic pessimism.[162] Human existence can be quite tolerable, at least momentarily, reaching at times a zero-ish point of almost no pain or anguish. The argument is that, in the absence of greater redeeming factors, even lives like this should not be created. Appealing to more popular intuitions, optimists like Anton can brush such feeble concerns aside.

The problem with all these quality-of-life claims is obvious. Only those who share these authors' aversion to the general bleakness of human existence agree with their conclusions. The sentiment is common among antinatalists – that is why they are antinatalists – but others remain unconvinced. Following Anton's lead, they can simply say that what Cabrera, Inmendham, Benatar, and Häyry call a burden is just what human life is, with its ups and downs, exhilarations and disappointments. We shall remedy this in the next section, but first two more attempts by Häyry need to be recounted.

Every human life can be expected to contain episodes of severe pain and anguish, a fact also well recognized by Inmendham and Benatar. One formulation of the risk argument for antinatalism uses this as a basis for questioning the rationality and morality of reproduction. If it is wrong to cause suffering, we should not bring about beings who suffer.[163] Rebuttals of the view have included the observation that episodes of suffering may make childbearing irrational but not immoral. There is more to morality than the avoidance of every fleeting pain.[164] It has also been suggested that most of the damage can be averted by responsible parenting.[165]

We should note, in the name of conceptual clarity, that this is actually another quality-of-life consideration. It is associated with the notion of risk only for historical reasons. Häyry – who did not use the term "risk argument" – presented two objections to childbearing together, in one package, and David Wasserman's qualified defense of pronatalism a decade later seems to have sealed the connection.[166]

Some human lives can be expected to be truly miserable, a fact verified in a legal sense by successful wrongful life cases.[167] Another formulation of the risk argument for antinatalism states that the mere possibility of such lives should give us pause in our reproductive endeavors.[168] Not only is the gift we are conferring bleak but it can also be devastatingly harmful. Even assuming that human existence can be good for some, to give a new individual life is like giving a stranger a bag full of either jewels or explosives. A cautious person would be wary of making such a donation.[169]

This, unlike the first version, is genuinely about risk. A miserable life is a possibility, not (like a life with some suffering) a certainty. Judging by the responses, however, caution is not popular among pronatalist ethicists. The stock objection is that lives should be lived according to outcomes that can be reasonably expected. A miserable existence is in most cases just an abstract fear.[170]

Anton's optimistic life-enthusiasm appeals to potential reproducers, and understandably so. They have, after all, more than half-resolved to have children even before the choice – if any – presents itself to them. The antinatalist case, to get through, would have to be very clear and to the point. Although we (the authors) understand and appreciate the arguments from lack of consent, manipulation, low quality of life, and risk, the reality is that something in them has, at least so far, prevented them from gaining widespread acclaim. In the following sections, we try to clarify the message.

3.2 Wrong and Right Outlined in Terms of Need Frustration

We begin by presenting the core views that we hold on what is wrong and what is right. From here on, the exposition is positional. These are the axioms that we accept, explained in the way we understand them. They do not define an entire moral theory. They explicate our main intuitions on what we see as focal to the natalism debate. These caveats notwithstanding, the principles are not controversial. Their application may be a different matter, but we shall get to that later.

Our partial definitions, with explanations below, are as follows (the rather technical language is necessary for the validity of our ensuing argument):[171]

Definitions
- It is prima facie wrong, deliberately or negligently, to bring about, or contribute to bringing about, legitimate fundamental need frustration.
- It is prima facie right to remove or to alleviate fundamental need frustration.

Explanations
- *Prima facie.* Choices may have several wrongdoing and rightdoing elements. If so, these must be balanced separately, in the light of other factors and intuitions.[172]
- *Wrong.* If the need frustration is the agent's own, the action is prudentially wrong; if somebody else's, it is morally wrong. Legal wrongness is a separate matter that we shall not consider here. To illustrate the difference, law may have to stop at reproductive autonomy and leave choices to individual citizens but that does not remove the moral "sin" of procreative wrongdoing (if any).
- *Deliberately or negligently.* If the agent genuinely does not know about the subsequent need frustration; cannot be reasonably expected to know; or makes an honest mistake, no wrong is done. This implies that all those who would like to prevent wrongdoing would be well advised to make the possibility of the specific wrongdoing known.
- *Bringing about something.* This primarily means acting so that the "something" is produced either as a result (immediate, intrinsic to the act) or as a consequence (mediated, extrinsic to the act). Deliberate or negligent omissions are also a way of bringing about. The first step in analyses of wrong and right could be to demonstrate the causation between the agent's act or omission and the result or consequence.
- *Contribute to bringing about* something. The wrongness persists even if the agent's act or omission would not, alone, bring about the frustration if it is brought about by the agent's act or omission combined with the reasonably

expected acts and omissions of others. A possible second step would be to show how the combination can be reasonably expected to produce the result or consequence.
- *Legitimate.* The frustration is not legitimate if the agent's need satisfaction would frustrate the legitimate fundamental needs of others. The third step would be to convince potential wrongdoers that if their needs can only be satisfied by wrongdoing, they do not count.[173]
- *Fundamental need frustration.* This is a comparative concept in that a frustration can be more fundamental than another but less fundamental than yet another. Some of the most widely recognized need frustrations are, however, symptomized by severe pain, deep anguish, and an irredeemable sense of helplessness.[174] The fourth step would be to sketch the nature of the reasonably expected need frustration that results or follows from the agent's – and possibly others' – acts or omissions.
- *Right.* If there are no wrongdoing factors present, it is always right to remove or to alleviate fundamental need frustration. If this can be done in many alternative ways, these must be balanced separately, in the light of other factors and intuitions.[175]

There is no natural way to encapsulate the entire contents of the definitions and explanations in a snappy catchphrase. But the main point for our present purpose is: do not bring about, or contribute to bringing about, severe pain, deep anguish, or an irredeemable sense of helplessness to some unless this is the only way to remove or alleviate the severe pain, deep anguish, or irredeemable sense of helplessness of others *and* a separate analysis in the light of other factors and intuitions supports it! Admittedly, not snappy, but it will get the job done as we move along.

3.3 The Ones Who Create *Omelas*

The argument from risk, recognized as one of the most intuitive defenses of antinatalism, suffers from a dilemma-type problem. Either the planned life is not miserable enough to warrant a duty to abstain; or, if it is, its probability is too small to be taken seriously. We believe that we have a solution to this problem.

In 1973, Ursula K. Le Guin published a short science fiction story titled *The Ones Who Walked Away from Omelas*.[176] It is about a utopian town where everybody is happy and there is no injustice, only eternal bliss. Except that, to uphold the serenity, the townspeople have to keep one child in perpetual filth, darkness, and misery. When the citizens are old enough to know the truth, the child is shown to them. After the initial shock, most of them accept the situation; some, as signaled in the title, walk away.

Le Guin's setting for *Omelas* has precedents in philosophy and literature. William James used the idea of a lost soul sacrificed for the good of the rest to illustrate the principle that no society should rest on the agony of its weakest members.[177] Fyodor Dostoevsky also raised the question in *The Brothers Karamazov* as an introduction to some deep theological reflections.[178] In both James and Dostoevsky, the fate of the unfortunate is presented as a choice. Given the chance, would you create such a world? In Le Guin's fable, people can only accept and stay; or reject and walk away.

Recently, Le Guin's *Omelas* has been linked with antinatalism.[179] The connection is not immediately clear. Reproducers could, of course, bring into existence a child whose life would be miserable, but they could also create children with happy lives. Their decision does not seem to bear an obvious resemblance to the choice of the Omelans. With some help from Dostoevsky and James, however, a feasible parallel can be drawn.

Le Guin's graphic image of the one lonely, frightened child in misery is indubitably more attention-grabbing than the abstractions relied on by her predecessors. But to link her case to procreation, we need James and Dostoevsky's idea of making ourselves responsible for the scenario. Would you, given the opportunity, create *Omelas*? There is reason to believe that reproducers would. In fact, every time they bear a child, they do. How they do it needs some explaining, though.

Our explanation is based on a reminder of the full consequences of having children. The second – genuine – version of the risk argument states that since the new lives could be miserable, bringing them into existence would be wrong. The standard pronatalist response is that if proper precautions are taken, the risk is very small and can be ignored. This, while possibly true regarding the children of the current reproducers, fails to account for the temporal dimension. The mistake is understandable given the notion of risk normally in use. The error becomes visible, however, when the reiterative nature of procreation is brought to the fore.

Opponents of the risk argument tend to think in terms of just one generation. There is a danger that my child's life turns out to be bad; but if I can avert this danger, all is well and my reproductive project is safe. But, as far as my choice is concerned, my children will also have children, who will have children, and so on ad infinitum. And after a sufficient number of reiterations during the next decades, centuries, and millennia, with certainty, someone will have a miserable life. That someone is the *Omelas* child. That child is required for the happiness of everyone else in between and beyond. And this is how my decision to have one child makes me the one who creates *Omelas*.

3.4 An Argument from Reiteration and the Procreator's Dilemma

Spelling out the obvious, the last two sections have laid the foundations for an argument against reproduction, based on the reiterative nature of continued procreation and our view on what is wrong. If (or, for us, because[180]) it is prima facie morally wrong to bring about, or contribute to bringing about, severe pain, deep anguish, or an irredeemable sense of helplessness, and since an unbroken chain of childbearing will eventually produce an individual experiencing these, it is prima facie morally wrong to procreate. Potential reproducers, it seems, morally corrupt themselves by becoming creators of their own personal *Omelas*.

Our story does not stop here – there is more to come. But before we go on, let us touch briefly upon two obvious objections. There will be those who say that the *Omelas* child will never happen in their family line; and there will be those who say that the misery of some is an unavoidable – and in the absence of better solutions acceptable – part of human life. Those who deny their own *Omelas* are mistaken. If reproduction goes on in their family lines for millennia, a truly horrible life will eventually be produced, however strict the criterion for sufficient horror is. Those who accept the sacrifice draw on the feelings and attitudes of people who do not think. We shall deal with them shortly.

For now, on with the story. Our argument, if accepted, places procreators, parents, in the horns of a dilemma. In one horn, they can still avoid creating their *Omelas* by convincing their children or grandchildren not to reproduce. If these fruits of their loins are healthy and happy, and if the chain ends in them, the envisioned harm will not materialize. This does not mean that the procreators are off the hook, though. Transferring the decision to break the chain to one's progeny may be morally less wrong than contributing to the creation of the *Omelas* child, but it burdens the progeny with something that could be called an antinatalist imposition.

In the excerpts that we cited, Anton alludes to another kind of imposition, one that antinatalists allegedly force upon the unborn. This is disingenuous. As long as there is no one in existence, there is no one who could be imposed upon. Language does tricks here and the truth is difficult to formulate. If we say that the ones who do not exist cannot consent, we are already giving "them" a kind of proto-existence. This should be avoided. The actual antinatalist imposition is forced by parents upon their (by then existing) children. The phenomenon has not been systematically studied but there are reproducers who have become antinatalists after becoming parents and their testimonies are telling. Here is one of them, Danny Shine, on the topic:

> I make it clear to them that I do not want them to have children. I do not want to be a grandfather; I do not want them to be burdened with children. And it's hard for them, they have to work it out themselves obviously, they're going to do whatever they do, whether I want it or not. But I try to explain to them as often as I can why I've got that position, and it's tough for them, and they have to make up their own minds. In some ways, it's a very depressing idea because it it's like throwing water on the fire of hope.[181]

The agony of the (by now irreversible) procreative self-corruption and the imposition of the choice upon the offspring is palpable. The decision to have children is not psychologically easy to overturn by making the next generation responsible for breaking the chain.

In the other horn of the dilemma, parents do not tell their children about the dangers of reproduction. The mentally difficult antinatalist imposition is avoided but two morally worse scenarios loom large. As far as the parents are concerned, the eventual birth of the *Omelas* child is allowed in this alternative. In addition, procreators are self-coerced into imposing upon their offspring a pronatalist mentality and lifestyle. The children will in time hear, as did the parents, about the dire consequences of procreation. No actual antinatalist imposition is needed for that, Anton's claims notwithstanding. In an open society, the knowledge will reach them without any manipulation when they are mature enough to seek information and to make autonomous decisions based on it. The mentality and the lifestyle are needed to inoculate the young against the message when they hear it.

We have presented and defended the argument from the postnatal mental imposition elsewhere,[182] and will return to some of its features here, but before that, let us see what rationalizations and moralizations pronatalists can come up with when faced with the procreator's dilemma.

3.5 The One, the Many, and Meaning Cocreated

When confronted with standard antinatalist arguments, pronatalists typically defend themselves – like Anton does in the excerpts cited – with a comparative approach. Not all lives are bad and ordinary risks are acceptable considering the enormous benefits to the procreators, their children, families, communities, nations, cultures, and humankind.[183] The procreators attain personal fulfillment; children are usually healthy, happy, and glad they are alive; family lines are worth preserving; communities gain strength and resilience by having new members; nations need producers, consumers, and defenders; cultures are a valuable source of identity; and the demise of the species would be unthinkable.

The success of the comparative approach depends on the arguments it is responding to. The benefit considerations would be quite formidable against a positive utilitarian case for antinatalism, which states that the greatest happiness of the greatest number will be achieved by ceasing to reproduce. It is just that antinatalism is seldom defended on positive utilitarian grounds. Negative utilitarian, yes; Kantian, yes; but positive utilitarian, no. That would be self-defeating.

Directed against our view – which prima facie prohibits fundamental and legitimate need frustration – the comparative defense shows its main weakness. The one or the few are sacrificed for the good of the many. This has been the insurmountable stumbling block of consequentialist ethics for decades.[184] Using a fictional character, Mr. Spock – the overly rational half-human, half-Vulcan science officer of Starship Enterprise in the Star Trek series – does sacrifice himself to save the lives of his crew mates, and gives birth to the statement, "The needs of the many outweigh the needs of the few, or the one."[185] Whatever we think about Mr. Spock's logic, it does not apply to the creators of *Omelas*. They are not sacrificing themselves to benefit their families, communities, nations, or cultures. They are sacrificing the eventual *Omelas* child to benefit others and, what is even more sinister, themselves.

It should be noted that a thinking person need not be an efilist or a negative utilitarian to understand the significance of suffering in reproductive choices. Christine Overall, a seminal feminist philosopher, illustrates this well in an interview:

> I am now completing an invited paper for a journal edition on David Benatar's anti-natalism. Benatar has famously argued that for every human being, it is better never to have been, and that therefore people have a duty not to have children. I criticized his ideas extensively in my book, *Why Have Children? The Ethical Debate*. Since then, I have become more convinced, on a visceral level, by one of his arguments for anti-natalism, namely, the argument from the sheer ubiquity and depth and variety of suffering.
>
> At the same time, however, I cannot bring myself to regret having two children, nor to feel guilty about having had them. Indeed, I cannot bring myself to believe that I was morally wrong in creating my own two children, now adults, nor that my children were morally wrong in each having two children of their own. And, this is in spite of my intense awareness, magnified now that I've lived for seventy-two years, of the depth and extent of human (and animal) suffering.
>
> Thus, the paper for the journal edition on Benatar's anti-natalism explores whether and how, if at all, I can justify, dissolve, or reconcile the apparent tension between my awareness of the power of Benatar's anti-natalist argument from suffering, and my belief that my children and their children – and indeed most other people – are not "better never to have been."[186]

Feminist thinkers are rare in the antinatalist camp – Patricia MacCormack being an outstanding exception – and Overall's doubts lend remarkable support to taking suffering seriously. Judging by her earlier references to her own children and their children in the interview, however, she may yet find a pronatalist solution; and it would not surprise us to see the solution anchored in one way or another in meaning in life.

Concerns about personal fulfillment, happiness, and meaning permeate contemporary Western culture. Popular media is eager to give visibility to the views of psychologists whose research confirms that children make parents happy or unhappy or provide or do not provide them with some deeper kind of satisfaction.[187] The child-related considerations are in a side role and the main outcome of reproduction is the happiness of the procreators. But here comes the trick. If having progeny gives meaning to parents' lives, there is every reason to expect that it will also give meaning to the children's lives, when they have children of their own. Note the words "when they have children." The "when" is crucially important.

Meaning in life can, as David Benatar, for one, has shown,[188] take a plethora of forms. We proceed from the elementary observation that while entities can normally be discovered or invented, the meaning of life can only be invented. No greater force has planted it into this world for us to find. Plato's demiurge, Augustine's creator, Aquinas's purpose giver, Berkeley's rule setter, and Leibnitz's clockmaker do not really exist. Plato, Augustine, Aquinas, Berkeley, and Leibnitz invented them, or borrowed them from others who had invented them. And even before they invented them, the ancient Greeks lamented the fact that someone had to do that. It would have been so much safer in a preordained world where we have an objectively meaningful role.

Since we do not have that, reproducers have spontaneously come up with an arrangement that averts the issue.[189] They have children, teach them to have children, and convince themselves and their children that this gives all their lives the objective, or at least intersubjective,[190] purpose required. A perfect, victimless self-deception. Except that there are two flies in the ointment.

Parents are now explicitly creating their own *Omelas* – or, more generally, contributing to bringing about suffering. They may not be doing it malevolently. As long as they would be happy to see the *Omelas* child not coming into existence *and* believe that the meaning created by the arrangement is real, the doctrine of double effect could protect them. Having children is, in their book, in and of itself morally good or at least neutral; they do not directly will or intend anyone to suffer; the happiness in their family line is not a consequence of the coming to being of sufferers; and the value of perpetuating procreative meaning is proportionally huge compared to some inevitable suffering.

However, when potential reproducers are made aware of their contribution to creating the *Omelas* child *and* of the self-invented nature of procreative meaning, they lose the support of the doctrine. Unless they completely refuse to think, following these revelations they should see that their quest is rather unbecomingly self-seeking. To put it bluntly, the egoism of aspiring parents is rationalized by rules that they themselves make up and uphold. This is not a solid basis for the requirement of proportionality. A child's suffering is not a minor concern when weighed against an insistence to make one's own existence bearable by playing by one's own rules.

Parents are also denying their children's freedom – and in a way that transcends their remit as responsible guardians. There are, of course, choices that procreators must make to ensure that their wards have the best possible lives;[191] or, as Jennifer Jackson would have it, a good standard of care.[192] In the light of their own understanding, they have to decide whether the child should take an early course in French; or have piano lessons; or engage in any number of other possible life-defining activities. On the surface, it may seem that teaching the child a pronatalist mentality is just one of these necessary yet innocuous interventions. A closer look reveals that this is not the case.

When children come of age, they can do what they like with their linguistic and musical skills. Adults regularly leave their French and Für Elise unused and it is quite easy to do so. The pronatalist mentality is of a different order. While shakable, barely, it holds most individuals in its grip with an irresistible force. This is why people still have children in an age that allows sex without pregnancies even between females and males. Technology enables child-free intercourse; and laws in many countries recognize the principle of reproductive freedom.

It should be noted that the wrongness of imposing the pronatalist mentality is separate from the wrongness of creating the *Omelas* child. Freedom has political connotations in liberal democracies; and one way to conceptualize the matter is through the notion of the child's right to an open future, used in debates on education and genetic selection.[193] By their actions, parents should not foreclose any reasonable and benign life decisions that their children grow up to make. In our language of right and wrong, we all have a need to make our choices autonomously, not dictated or molded by someone else's will.

By imposing a pronatalist mentality and lifestyle on their progeny, parents violate their children's right to an open future. In most cases, they do not explicitly force them to reproduce but they can and often do make the alternative highly unattractive.[194] This phenomenon has been identified by Julio Cabrera as a type of manipulation;[195] by David Benatar as a kind of indoctrination;[196] and by Heta Häyry as a form of unwarranted paternalism.[197]

The parental motivation to raise children in the spirit of pronatalism is understandable in many ways. Reproducers are proud to have offspring and want to see the cycle repeated in the next generation. The alternative, as shown by Danny Shine's example (Section 3.4), is not that tempting, either. Telling your children that having children is wrong comes close to saying that you regret their existence, that they are unwanted. Christine Overall may be expressing these concerns in her interview. Our solution to her problem, recognizing that the original sin of procreation is by this time irreversible, is that in discussions on natalism we call this year, "Year Zero." We return to this in our concluding, practically oriented section (Section 3.6). Guilt and shame may have their place in forward-looking considerations but they are an unnecessary burden when analyzing the situation of repentant sinners.

3.6 Routes to Ending Procreative Self-Corruption

There is a natural, practical objection to all of our normative reflections. Critics could argue that none of our conclusions can realistically lead to action. Even if the force of suffering and freedom in our sense were admitted, what we have built is just another philosophical castle in the air. People will continue having children, as is their biological and social nature, and only unnecessary fear and anxiety can be produced by spreading antinatalist ideas. Our own insistence that we should not contribute to bringing about pain and anguish turns against us.

Critics who say this do have a point. Reproductive urges are deeply rooted in human minds and they offer strong resistance to any attempts to halt procreation. Also, as David Benatar has shown in his meticulous treatment of phased extinction, an ever-dwindling population would experience hardships that make the consistent application of antinatalist principles challenging.[198] The gap between what we (the authors) would like to happen and what can happen is real. Since the moral stakes are high, however, some kind of a start is called for. We propose, therefore, a more positive, if conditional, approach to the matter. At the risk of reinventing the wheel, we conclude by analyzing the main possibilities for ending reproduction voluntarily; and we do it in the context of an overarching thought experiment.

Imagine that the following has happened. People have momentarily come to the conviction that by having children they commit an irredeemable moral wrong. We do not need precise knowledge of the nature of the moral wrong. Maybe they have become convinced of our arguments. The wrong is, however, serious enough to warrant decisive action, despite known hindrances and objections. Consequently, people have decided to end reproduction, although they know that the will to have progeny is strong and that universal abstinence would lead to the extinction of the species.

In this situation, accepting these premises, what should people do to achieve their goal? How could they end human reproduction safely and efficiently? Or are there other options that deserve to be considered? At least thirteen alternatives (there may be more) present themselves (the color code of the Buttons is partly ours):

- The Big Yellow Button: technological removal of suffering.
- The Big Orange Button: immortality by biomedical gerontology.
- The Big Red Button: obliteration of humankind.
- The Big Violet Button: emigration to virtual reality.
- The Big Blue Button: irreversible collective infertility.
- The Big Green Button: humankind makes room for other species.
- Antinatalist super/wo/men.
- Antinatalist dictatorship.
- Antinatalist cult or religion.
- Antinatalist liberal democracy.
- Rational persuasion.
- Cunning of reason.
- Benevolent machine.

Some of the options are more readily understandable than others. Let us describe them all briefly and evaluate their pros and cons, one by one.

The Big Yellow Button, an alternative rather than instrument of antinatalism, has been touched upon in our narrative as David Pearce's "Hedonistic Imperative." We could, according to him, remove all suffering from the world and live and breed on in unimaginable bliss.[199] The realism of technology saving the day like this aside, this solution leaves the question of imposition unanswered and does not end reproduction as expected by the suddenly enlightened humankind. We only include it here because some antinatalists who are wary of human extinction seem to find consolation in it.

The Big Orange Button is a partial answer to the concern over extinction. People cease to reproduce but biomedical gerontology keeps them alive indefinitely, unless they fall prey to violence or accidents.[200] This could alleviate worries about the demise of the species and thereby make the antireproductive project easier to implement, albeit that the life extension would be only temporary and that the promise of medicine's power is remarkably optimistic.

The Big Red Button is the bluntest tool in the box for those who just want to end procreation, not life. As noted, philosophers tend to avoid answering the question "Would you press?" because it is obvious that different theories produce different responses. Our normative view embraces the devise as a specific thought experiment. The philosopher half of the authorship would like to have people's consent to act – but in our wider thought experiment we have that. Reality is a different matter, as we shall see in the policy part of our list (beginning with the bullet point "Antinatalist super/wo/men").

The Big Violet Button would transfer us to virtual reality and remove the need for biological reproduction. In Section 2, we mentioned the problem of understanding what mind uploading and the ensuing virtual life would entail. With our normative view, we can add the concern that computer existence could also contain pain and anguish. Since "emigrating" to the virtual world would probably mean killing ourselves and giving immaterial birth to someone else, we would create a new individual who possibly suffers, which would be against our idea of wrongdoing.

The Big Blue Button is one of the most realistic devises on our list. It is just about imaginable that contraceptives could be added to food and drink everywhere, making everyone infertile.[201] People who shun sudden human extinction might be more attracted to this solution than something more abrupt. In real life, the pain and anguish involved would speak against the decision. Within our thought experiment, if people want it, they can have it.

The Big Green Button would be the solution suggested by Patricia MacCormack.[202] Humankind radically changes its attitude toward other species and the natural environment and starts making amends for past crimes against them. The details are a little blurry, but the general idea is that humans stop procreating, die away, and leave the planet to others – in the best shape possible. The activist half of the authorship notes that this leaves nonhuman suffering unaddressed; the philosopher half would settle for leaving the fate of other species to their own self-direction.[203]

Antinatalist super/wo/men would be exceptional persons who further the cause in exceptional ways. In our contemporary world, they could be militants, even saboteurs or terrorists, secretly building Red or Blue Buttons. Some activists may already have sharpened their swords, but we have premonitions of a misinterpreted Nietzschean *Übermensch*. In our imaginary framework, however, such individuals could well be appointed by the people to secure the success of the project they know may have to face even their own resistance.

Antinatalist dictatorship would be a logical conclusion if the superheroes decided to go rogue and crush opposition in the name of the greater good. Even within the thought experiment, this arrangement would have its problems. Dictatorships are not known for their long-term stability and people's opposition might be detrimental to achieving the initial aim. Some people could actually turn against the plan if it were forced upon them.

Antinatalist cult or religion is a slightly softer alternative to dictatorship. Knowing people's hunger for magic and rituals, it could be a palatable route. The sect or faith would not, at least initially, have to operate under the threat that Gnostics had to endure in the Roman Empire. On the other hand, in a secularized world, some distaste and aversion would have to be expected. Our imaginary people came to a momentary revelation about the wrongness of reproduction, not to a sudden dedication to a new faith system.

Antinatalist liberal democracy is the most natural solution for modern people who have decided to stop having children. It is, unlike a dictatorship or a cult, politically acceptable and ideologically neutral. Its obvious downside is the commitment to respecting the will of citizens even if they choose to overturn their original decision. The recognition of the urge to procreate could easily be its undoing.

Rational persuasion is a solution dictated by our own premises. Imposing an antinatalist mentality upon populations could spell an end to creating *Omelas* children but it would assault human freedom in a way that our argument precludes. Persuasion is the route we are on. In the thought experiment, we could emphasize that it is indeed "Year Zero" of antinatalism. People have the children they have and we are only trying to convince them not to have any more now that they know, thanks to our articulation, about the wrongness of procreation. Perhaps within an antinatalist liberal democracy this conviction could be developed into a civic virtue and a source of pride.

Cunning of reason refers to the hope that the world is guided by a principle that, despite individual human actions, leads to the best possible result, in this case childlessness. For instance, chemical pollution caused by our current lifestyle could lead to a rapid lowering of sperm counts and – eventually – to universal infertility.

Benevolent machine is a technological variant of the cunning of reason. Perhaps Thomas Metzinger is correct, and a kind and all-powerful computer is already preparing a Button that will solve our problems and end procreative self-corruption.[204] That would be an unexpected – but for us welcome – surprise.

These are some of the options that humankind would have if it decided to change things, and they need to be further developed to effect an antinatalist upheaval. There are practical problems to be solved and it is more than likely that nothing like this will happen during our lifetime, if ever. But if our normative considerations are valid, the moral side cannot and need not be ignored. By not having (any or more) children, every one of us can make a difference. The old Jewish saying has it that "Whosoever saves a single life, saves an entire universe." For the living, this can be taken as read. Save lives, remove suffering. For the unborn, the wording could be: "Whosoever refuses to create a single life, saves an entire moral universe." It is an aspiration.

Notes

1. Nietzsche 2000 [1872], 124.
2. Antinatalism 2023.
3. *Larousse* no date; *Le Robert* no date.
4. Akerma 2017, 2021.
5. Lochmanová 2020.
6. de Giraud 2021.
7. Morioka 2021.
8. Coates 2014.
9. Copleston 1946, 17–18; Nietzsche 2000 [1872].
10. Plutarch 1928, 181.
11. Theognis 425–28 (cited by Gerber 1999, 234); Sophocles 2000; Euripides 2020.
12. Anaxagoras (cited by Barnes 2001, 190).
13. Thales of Miletus (cited by Lochmanová 2020, 42).
14. Sukenick 2023a.
15. Berryman 2023.
16. Democritus [B 275] (IV xxiv 29) (cited by Barnes 2001, 245). As Barnes (p. xxxv) explains, "the fragments are equipped with 'Diels-Kranz numbers' (these are the ciphers which appear in square brackets after the text). The numbers key the passages to the standard edition of the Greek texts, edited by Hermann Diels and Walther Kranz: *Die Fragments Der Vorsokratiker.*"
17. Democritus [B 276] (IV xxiv 30) (cited by Barnes 2001, 245).
18. Democritus [B 277] (IV xxiv 30) (cited by Barnes 2001, 245).
19. Democritus [B 278] (IV xxiv 31) (cited by Barnes 2001, 245).
20. Kraut 1992, 32.
21. Brown 2017.
22. Afnan 1969.
23. Häyry 2008.
24. Häyry 2008.
25. Häyry 2008.
26. Coates 2014.
27. Häyry 2008; Kraut 2022; Miller 2022.
28. Konstan 2022; Durand, Shogry, & Baltzly 2023.
29. Lucretius 2001.
30. Warren 2004.
31. Cicero 2022, 31.
32. Seneca 2017 [1917].
33. Letter 47 (cited by Malherbe 1977, 179).
34. de Giraud 2021.
35. Matthew 24:9–11, 15–19 (in Sukenick 2023b).
36. Green 2021; Shead 2021; Williams 2021.

37. Yarbrough 1986, 108 (cited by McKeown 2014, xxx).
38. 1 Corinthians 7:8–9 (in Sukenick 2023b).
39. Sukenick 2023b.
40. Pagels 1979.
41. Arendzen 1913.
42. Hippolytus (cited by Arendzen 1913).
43. Doniger 1999, 689–90.
44. Tornau 2020.
45. Doniger 1999, 689–90.
46. Morioka 2021, 9–12.
47. Romans 13:13–14 (in Sukenick 2023b).
48. McKeown 2014, 151.
49. Coyle 2003 (cited by McKeown 2014).
50. McKeown 2014, 151.
51. Tornau 2020.
52. Asimov 1950 [1942], 40.
53. Wilson 2018, 16–18, 157–59, 269–71, 279–85.
54. Al-Ma'arri (cited by Hastings 1909, 190).
55. Al-Ma'arri (cited by Maalouf 1984, 37).
56. Al-Ma'arri (cited by Blankinship 2015).
57. Al-Ma'arri (cited by Nicholson 1921, 139).
58. Al-Ma'arri (cited by Nicholson 1921, 139).
59. Al-Ma'arri (cited by Nicholson 1921, 139).
60. Al-Ma'arri (cited by Nicholson 1921, 140).
61. Al-Ma'arri (cited by Nicholson 1921, 139).
62. Nicholson 1921.
63. Crampton 2005, 18–19; Rist 2015.
64. Rist 2015.
65. Pasnau 2023.
66. Ben Ahmed & Pasnau 2021.
67. Aquinas 2017 [1920].
68. Alighieri IV, 33–42 (in Barolini, 2018).
69. Fabian 2019; International Theological Commission 2007.
70. Baranski 2020.
71. Häyry 1994.
72. Häyry & Häyry 1994; Häyry 2012.
73. Häyry 1994.
74. Look 2020.
75. Johnson no date.
76. Takala & Häyry 2023.
77. Schultz 2021.
78. Häyry & Häyry 1998.
79. Sukenick 2023a.
80. Häyry 2010; 2017; 2018.
81. Häyry 2010.
82. Jackson 2006, 187.

83. Oderberg 2000, 47.
84. Scruton 2006, 83.
85. Schopenhauer 2007 [1851], 8.
86. Mill 1996 [1859], 104.
87. Savulescu 2001, 415.
88. Narveson 1967, 70–71.
89. Parfit 1984.
90. Häyry 1994, 121.
91. Anscombe 1989.
92. Smart 1958.
93. Smart & Williams 1973, 29.
94. Häyry 2002; 2007; 2021; 2023a.
95. Narveson 1988.
96. Benatar 1997.
97. Shiffrin 1999.
98. The Exploring Antinatalism Podcast 2022b, 22:45–24:32.
99. Häyry 2004a; Benatar & Wasserman 2015.
100. Benatar 2006, 164, 199.
101. Häyry 2023a.
102. Akerma 2000, 17 (trans. Karim Akerma).
103. Sukenick 2023a.
104. Sartre 2000 [1938]; Camus 1991 [1942].
105. Kurnig 1903, 84 (trans. Karim Akerma).
106. Zapffe 2004 [1933].
107. Haave 1999 (cited by Hickman 2022).
108. Fukuyama 1992.
109. The Voluntary Human Extinction Movement 1996; Jarvis 1994.
110. efilist 2011.
111. Pearce 1995.
112. Pearce 2018.
113. Pearce 2018.
114. Anton 2021, 31:11–31:51.
115. Häyry 2023b.
116. Jones 1985, 1.
117. Metzinger 2017.
118. Chomanski 2021.
119. Morioka 2021, 23.
120. Benatar 2006, 83.
121. Benatar 2006, 136.
122. Bentham 1982 [1789], 283.
123. Benatar 2006, 223.
124. Akerma 2023.
125. Häyry 2023a.
126. The Graphene Rule 2020.
127. Sukenick 2016.
128. Häyry 2023a.

129. Savulescu 2001.
130. Mill 1996 [1859], 104.
131. McIntyre 2019.
132. Kant 1998 [1785], 38.
133. Cabrera 2018; 2019.
134. Akerma 2023; Häyry 2023a.
135. Ashcroft 2009, 186; Häyry 1994; 1999; 2004a.
136. Pearce 1995, section 0.4.
137. Häyry 2022; Häyry & Laihonen 2022; Takala & Häyry 2023.
138. Anton 2021, 32:23–33:25.
139. Harris 2003.
140. Harris 2003.
141. de Grey 1999; de Grey & Rae 2007; Häyry 2010, 195–219; 2011.
142. MacCormack 2020, 154.
143. MacCormack 2020, 168–69.
144. Puka no date.
145. Jollimore 2017.
146. Williams 2023.
147. Anton 2021, 149–54.
148. The Exploring Antinatalism Podcast #72 2023, 18:32–19:24.
149. Inmendham Videos 2018, 32:23–32:56.
150. The Exploring Antinatalism Podcast #72 2023, 54:38–54:55.
151. GloomBoomDoom 2011, 12:22–16:06.
152. Anton 2021, 149–54.
153. MacCormack 2020.
154. Shiffrin 1999; Häyry & Sukenick 2023, 8.
155. Anton 2021, 150.
156. Cabrera 1996; 2011 [1989]; 2019, 126–38.
157. Cabrera 2020, 176.
158. SufferingSucks 2011.
159. Question Mark? Philosophy 2021.
160. Anti Natalism 2012.
161. Benatar 2006, 61.
162. Häyry 2024.
163. Häyry 2004a.
164. Bennett 2004.
165. Weinberg 2016.
166. Benatar & Wasserman 2015.
167. Bayne 2013.
168. Häyry 2004a.
169. Häyry 2004b.
170. Magnusson 2022.
171. Häyry 2015a.
172. Häyry 1994; 2021; 2023a.
173. Häyry 2023a.
174. Häyry 2023a.

175. Häyry 1994; 2021; 2023a.
176. Le Guin 1973.
177. James 2006 [1891].
178. Dostoyevsky 2003 [1879–1880].
179. Life Sucks 2019; Woolfe 2020; Anton 2022; The Exploring Antinatalism Podcast 2022a; Contestabile 2023; Antinatalism no date.
180. Häyry 2015b.
181. The Exploring Antinatalism Podcast #22 2020, 42:36–45:33.
182. Häyry & Sukenick 2023.
183. Häyry 2023c.
184. Häyry 2021.
185. Meyer 1982. To be precise, the scene is a dialogue. Mr. Spock: "Logic clearly dictates that the needs of the many outweigh the needs of the few." Captain Kirk: "Or the one."
186. Tremain 2021.
187. Margolis & Myrskylä 2011; Bloom 2021; Rotondo 2022; Burnett 2023.
188. Benatar 2017.
189. Häyry & Sukenick 2023.
190. Häyry 2005.
191. Weinberg 2016.
192. Jackson 2006.
193. Feinberg 1992, 76–97; Davis 1997; Takala 2003; Häyry & Sukenick 2023.
194. Häyry & Sukenick 2023.
195. Cabrera 1996; 2009; 99; 2011 [1989].
196. Benatar 1997, 352.
197. Häyry 1991, 119.
198. Benatar 2006, 182ff.
199. Pearce 1995.
200. de Grey 1999; de Grey & Rae 2007; Häyry 2010, 195–219; 2011.
201. Efil Blaise 2022.
202. MacCormack 2020.
203. Häyry 2023a.
204. Metzinger 2017.

References

Afnan, Rubi Muhsen. *Zoroaster's Influence on Anaxagoras, the Greek Tragedians, and Socrates*. New York: Philosophical Library, 1969.

Akerma, Karim. *Verebben der Menschheit?: Neganthropie und Anthropodizee*. Freiburg: Verlag Karl Alber, 2000.

Akerma, Karim. *Antinatalismus: Ein Handbuch*. Berlin: Epubli, 2017.

Akerma, Karim. *Antinatalism: A Handbook*. Berlin: Epubli, 2021.

Akerma, Karim. On Matti Häyry's "Exit Duty Generator." *Cambridge Quarterly of Healthcare Ethics*. Published online March 24, 2023. https://doi.org/10.1017/S0963180123000142.

Anscombe, G. E. M. Why Have Children? *Proceedings of the American Catholic Philosophical Association* 63 (1989): 48–53.

Anti Natalism. Inmendham vs Professor Anton Debate – TheModernMystic. Online video clip. July 13, 2012. www.youtube.com/watch?v=2JOY4i-BCTE.

Antinatalism. *Wikipedia*. June 10, 2023. https://en.wikipedia.org/wiki/Antinatalism.

Anton, Corey. *How Non-Being Haunts Being: On Possibilities, Morality, and Death Acceptance*. Madison, NJ: The Fairleigh Dickinson University Press, 2021.

Anton, Lawrence. Should Humans Go Extinct?|Debate. Online video clip. June 20, 2021. www.youtube.com/watch?v=4pafyDEofHg&t=4191s.

Anton, Lawrence. The Ones Who Walk Away from Natalism. Online video clip. October 9, 2022. www.youtube.com/watch?v=cHRD3AY8Qbg.

Aquinas, Thomas. *Summa Theologica*. Second and revised edition [1920]. Online edition by Kevin Knight, 2017. www.newadvent.org/summa/3153.htm#article2.

Arendzen, John Peter. Encratites. In Charles Herbermann, ed. *Catholic Encyclopedia*, Volume 5. New York: Robert Appleton Company, 1913: 1073–75.

Ashcroft, Richard. Is It Irrational to Have Children? In Tuija Takala, Peter Herissone-Kelly, and Soren Holm, eds. *Cutting Through the Surface: Philosophical Approaches to Bioethics*. Amsterdam: Rodopi, 2009: 183–95.

Asimov, Isaac. Runaround [1942]. In Isaac Asimov, *I, Robot*. New York: Doubleday, 1950.

Baranski, Zygmunt G. *Dante, Petrarch, Boccaccio: Literature, Doctrine, Reality*. Cambridge: Legenda, 2020.

Barnes, Jonathan. *Early Greek Philosophy*. Harmondsworth: Penguin Books, 2001.

Barolini, Teodolinda. *Inferno* 4: Non-Christians in the Christian Afterlife. Commento Baroliniano, Digital Dante. New York: Columbia University Libraries, 2018. https://digitaldante.columbia.edu/dante/divine-comedy/inferno/inferno-4/.

Bayne, Tim. Wrongful Life. In Hugh LaFollette, ed. *The International Encyclopedia of Ethics*. 2013. https://doi.org/10.1002/9781444367072.wbiee272.

Ben Ahmed, Fouad, and Pasnau, Robert. Ibn Rushd [Averroes]. In Edward N. Zalta, ed. *The Stanford Encyclopedia of Philosophy*. 2021. https://plato.stanford.edu/archives/fall2021/entries/ibn-rushd.

Benatar, David. Why It Is Better Never to Come into Existence. *American Philosophical Quarterly* 34 (1997): 345–55.

Benatar, David. *Better Never to Have Been*. Oxford: Clarendon, 2006.

Benatar, David. *The Human Predicament: A Candid Guide to Life's Biggest Questions*. Oxford: Oxford University Press, 2017.

Benatar, David, and Wasserman, David. *Debating Procreation: Is It Wrong to Reproduce?* Oxford: Oxford University Press, 2015.

Bennett, Rebecca. Human Reproduction: Irrational But in Most Cases Morally Defensible. *Journal of Medical Ethics* 30 (2004): 379–80.

Bentham, Jeremy. *An Introduction to the Principles of Morals and Legislation* [1789]. Edited by J. H. Burns and H. L. A. Hart. London: Methuen, 1982.

Berryman, Sylvia. Democritus. In Edward N. Zalta and Uri Nodelman, eds. *The Stanford Encyclopedia of Philosophy*. 2023. https://plato.stanford.edu/archives/spr2023/entries/democritus/.

Blankinship, Kevin. An Elegy by al-Ma'arri. *Jadaliyya*. September 20, 2015. www.jadaliyya.com/Details/32488.

Bloom, Paul. What Becoming a Parent Really Does to Your Happiness. *The Atlantic*. November 2, 2021. www.theatlantic.com/family/archive/2021/11/does-having-kids-make-you-happy/620576/.

Brown, Eric. Plato's Ethics and Politics in *The Republic*. In Edward N. Zalta, ed. *The Stanford Encyclopedia of Philosophy*. 2017. https://plato.stanford.edu/archives/fall2017/entries/plato-ethics-politics/.

Burnett, Dean. Does Having Children Actually Make You Happy? A Neuroscientist Explains. *BBC Science Focus*. May 14, 2023. www.sciencefocus.com/the-human-body/does-having-kids-make-you-happy.

Cabrera, Julio. *Critica de La Moral Afirmativa: Una Reflexión Sobre Nacimiento, Muerte y Valor de La Vida*. Barcelona: Gedisa, 1996.

Cabrera, Julio. *A Ética e Suas Negações, Não nascer, suicídio e pequenos assassinatos* [1989]. Second edition. Rio de Janeiro: Rocco, 2011.

Cabrera, Julio. *Mal-estar e moralidade: Situação humana, ética e procriação responsável*. Brasilia: Editora Universidade de Brasilia, 2018.

Cabrera, Julio. *Discomfort and Moral Impediment: The Human Situation, Radical Bioethics and Procreation*. Newcastle upon Tyne: Cambridge Scholars Publishing, 2019.

Cabrera, Julio. Antinatalism and Negative Ethics. In Kateřina Lochmanová, ed. *History of Antinatalism: How Philosophy Has Challenged the Question of Procreation*. Monee, IL: Kateřina Lochmanová, 2020: 167–88.

Cabrera, Julio, and di Santis, Thiago Lenharo. *Porque te amo, Nao nasceras! Nascituri te salutant*. Brasilia: Editora LGE, 2009.

Camus, Albert. *The Myth of Sisyphus* [1942]. Translated by Justin O'Brien. New York: Vintage Books, 1991.

Chaliakopoulos, Antonis. What Is the Apollonian and Dionysian In Nietzsche's Philosophy? *The Collector*. January 13, 2022. www.thecollector.com/nietzsche-philosophy-apollonian-dionysian/.

Chomanski, Bartlomiej "Bartek." Anti-Natalism and the Creation of Artificial Minds. *Journal of Applied Philosophy* 38 (2021): 870–85.

Cicero, Marcus Tulles. *How to Grieve: An Ancient Guide to the Lost Art of Consolation*. Translated by Michael Fontaine. Princeton, NJ: Princeton University Press, 2022.

Coates, Ken. *Anti-Natalism: Rejectionist Philosophy from Buddhism to Benatar*. Sarasota, FL: Design Publishing, 2014.

Contestabile, Bruno. Antinatalism and the Minimization of Suffering. 2023. www.socrethics.com/Folder2/NU.htm.

Copleston, Frederick. *A History of Philosophy Volume 1: Greece and Rome*. Tunbridge Wells: Burns & Oates, 1946.

Coyle, J. Kevin. Saint Augustine's Manichean Legacy. In J. Kevin Coyle, *Manichaeism and Its Legacy*. Nag Hammadi and Manichaean Studies, Volume 69. Leiden: Brill, 2003: 307–10. https://brill.com/display/book/9789047429180/Bej.9789004175747.i-348_020.xml.

Crampton, Richard J. *A Concise History of Bulgaria*. Cambridge: Cambridge University Press, 2005.

Davis, Dena S. Genetic Dilemmas and the Child's Right to an Open Future. *Hastings Center Report* 27 (1997): 7–15.

de Giraud, Théophile. *The Childfree Christ: Antinatalism in Early Christianity*. Monee, IL: Théophile de Giraud, 2021.

de Grey, Aubrey. *The Mitochondrial Free Radical Theory of Aging*. Austin, TX: R. G. Landes Company, 1999.

de Grey, Aubrey, and Rae, Michael. *Ending Aging: The Rejuvenation Breakthroughs That Could Reverse Human Aging in Our Lifetime*. New York: St Martin's Press, 2007.

Doniger, Wendy. *Merriam-Webster's Encyclopedia of World Religions*. Springfield, MA: Merriam-Webster, 1999.

Dostoyevsky, Fyodor. *The Brothers Karamazov* [1879–1880]. Translated by Constance Gamett. New York: Penguin Classics, 2003.

Durand, Marion, Shogry, Simon, and Baltzly, Dirk. Stoicism. In Edward N. Zalta and Uri Nodelman, eds. *The Stanford Encyclopedia of Philosophy*. 2023. https://plato.stanford.edu/archives/spr2023/entries/stoicism/.

Efil Blaise. Efil studio with Oldphan#efilism #promortalism #extinction #antinatalism. Online video clip. October 29, 2022. www.youtube.com/watch?v=g9TDR-K0xh0.

efilist. Efilist 1. Online video clip. September 3, 2011. www.youtube.com/watch?v=1vzrpTE4geE.

Euripides. *Cyclops*. Edited by Richard Hunter and Rebecca Laemmle. Cambridge: Cambridge University Press, 2020.

Fabian, Seth. Dante and the Limbo of Unbaptized Infants. *The Scribe*, November 1, 2019. https://sjvlaydivision.org/dante-and-limbo/.

Feinberg, Joel. *Freedom and Fulfillment: Philosophical Essays*. Princeton, NJ: Princeton University Press, 1992.

Fukuyama, Francis. *The End of History and the Last Man*. New York: Free Press, 1992.

Gerber, Douglas E. *Greek Elegiac Poetry: From the Seventh to the Fifth Centuries B.C.* Cambridge, MA: Harvard University Press, 1999.

GloomBoomDoom. re: RE – Antinatalism as Dangerous Idea [anton]. Online video clip. July 1, 2011. www.youtube.com/watch?v=G2AIqXIsZac.

Green, Emma. A World without Children. *The Atlantic*, September 20, 2021. www.theatlantic.com/politics/archive/2021/09/millennials-babies-climate-change/620032/.

Haave, *Jørgen*. Naken under kosmos: Peter Wessel Zapffe, en biografi. Oslo: Pax, 1999.

Harris, John. Intimations of Immortality: The Ethics and Justice of Life-Extending Therapies. In M. D. A. Freeman, ed. *Current Legal Problems 2002*. Oxford: Oxford University Press, 2003: 65–95.

Hastings, James. *Encyclopedia of Religion and Ethics*, Vol. 2. Edinburgh: T&T Clark, 1909.

Häyry, Heta. *The Limits of Medical Paternalism*. London: Routledge, 1991.

Häyry, Heta, and Häyry, Matti. Applied Philosophy at the Turn of the Millennium. In Oliver Leaman, ed. *The Future of Philosophy: Towards the 21st Century*. London: Routledge, 1998: 90–104.

Häyry, Matti. *Liberal Utilitarianism and Applied Ethics*. London: Routledge, 1994. www.utilitarianism.com/liberal-utilitarianism.pdf.

Häyry, Matti. What the Fox Would Have Said, Had He Been a Hedgehog: On the Methodology and Normative Approach of John Harris's Wonderwoman and Superman. In Veikko Launis, Juhani Pietarinen, and Juha Räikkä, eds. *Genes and Morality: New Essays*. Amsterdam: Rodopi, 1999: 11–19.

Häyry, Matti. Utilitarian Approaches to Justice in Health Care. In Rosamond Rhodes, Margaret P. Battin, and Anita Silvers, eds. *Medicine and Social Justice: Essays on the Distribution of Health Care*. New York: Oxford University Press, 2002: 53–64.

Häyry, Matti. A Rational Cure for Prereproductive Stress Syndrome. *Journal of Medical Ethics* 20 (2004a): 377–78. https://doi.org/10.1136/jme.2003.004424.

Häyry, Matti. If You Must Make Babies, Then at Least Make the Best Babies You Can? *Human Fertility* 7 (2004b): 105–12. https://doi.org/10.1080/14647270410001699063.

Häyry, Matti. A Defense of Relativism. *Cambridge Quarterly of Healthcare Ethics* 14 (2005): 7–12. https://doi.org/10.1017/S0963180105050024.

Häyry, Matti. Utilitarianism and Bioethics. In Richard Ashcroft, Angus Dawson, Heather Draper, and John McMillan, eds. *Principles of Health Care Ethics*. Second edition. Chichester: John Wiley & Sons, 2007: 57–64.

Häyry, Matti. The Historical Idea of a Better Race. *Studies in Ethics, Law, and Technology* 2 (2008), article 11. https://doi.org/10.2202/1941-6008.1035.

Häyry, Matti. *Rationality and the Genetic Challenge*. Cambridge: Cambridge University Press, 2010.

Häyry, Matti. Considerable Life Extension and Three Views on the Meaning of Life. *Cambridge Quarterly of Healthcare Ethics* 20 (2011): 21–29. https://doi.org/10.1017/S0963180110000599.

Häyry, Matti. Passive Obedience and Berkeley's Moral Philosophy. *Berkeley Studies* 23 (2012): 3–14. https://bit.ly/47vKrWB.

Häyry, Matti. What Exactly Did You Claim? A Call for Clarity in the Presentation of Premises and Conclusions in Philosophical Contributions to Ethics. *Cambridge Quarterly of Healthcare Ethics* 24 (2015a): 107–12. https://doi.org/10.1017/S0963180114000358.

Häyry, Matti. What Do You Think of Philosophical Bioethics? *Cambridge Quarterly of Healthcare Ethics* 24 (2015b): 139–48. https://doi.org/10.1017/S0963180114000449.

Häyry, Matti. Synthetic Biology and Ethics: Past, Present, and Future. *Cambridge Quarterly of Healthcare Ethics* 26 (2017): 186–205. https://doi.org/10.1017/S0963180116000803.

Häyry, Matti. Ethics and Cloning. *British Medical Bulletin* 128 (2018): 15–21. https://doi.org/10.1093/bmb/ldy031.

Häyry, Matti. Just Better Utilitarianism. *Cambridge Quarterly of Healthcare Ethics* 30 (2021): 343–67. https://doi.org/10.1017/S0963180120000882.

Häyry, Matti. *Roles of Justice in Bioethics*. Cambridge: Cambridge University Press, 2022. https://doi.org/10.1017/9781009104364.

Häyry, Matti. Exit Duty Generator. *Cambridge Quarterly of Healthcare Ethics* (2023a): 1–15. https://doi.org/10.1017/S096318012300004X.

Häyry, Matti [under the pseudonym Polyester Carbogeddon]. Another Last Encounter: The Suppressed Case of Terran Panspermia. *Antinatalism International*, May 28, 2023b. https://bit.ly/3SaNkri.

Häyry, Matti. *Roe* v. *Wade* and the Predatory State Interest in Protecting Future Cannon Fodder. *Cambridge Quarterly of Healthcare Ethics* 32 (2023c): 434–42. https://doi.org/10.1017/S0963180122000342.

Häyry, Matti. If You Must Give Them a Gift, Then Give Them the Gift of Nonexistence. *Cambridge Quarterly of Healthcare Ethics* 33 (2024): 48–59. https://doi.org/10.1017/S0963180122000317.

Häyry, Matti, and Häyry, Heta. Obedience to Rules and Berkeley's Theological Utilitarianism. *Utilitas* 6 (1994): 233–42. https://doi.org/10.1017/S0953820800001618.

Häyry, Matti, and Laihonen, Maarit. Situating a Sustainable Bioeconomy Strategy on a Map of Justice: A Solution and Its Problems. *Environment, Development and Sustainability*. Published online October 21, 2022. https://doi.org/10.1007/s10668-022-02720-w.

Häyry, Matti, and Sukenick, Amanda. Imposing a Lifestyle: A New Argument for Antinatalism. *Cambridge Quarterly of Healthcare Ethics*. Published online July 27, 2023. https://doi.org/10.1017/S0963180123000385.

Hickman, S. C. Prelude to Abjection: Thomas Ligotti and Peter Wessel Zapffe. *The Dark Fantastic: Literature, Philosophy, and Digital Arts,* June 20, 2022. https://socialecologies.wordpress.com/2022/06/20/prelude-to-abjection-thomas-ligotti-and-peter-wessel-zapffe/.

Inmendham Videos. Dialogue 2 with Inmendham. Online video clip. March 6, 2018. www.youtube.com/watch?v=sUMQ53KdJGo.

References

International Theological Commission. The Hope of Salvation for Infants Who Die Without Being Baptized. *Catholic Culture*, January 19, 2007. www.catholicculture.org/culture/library/view.cfm?id=7529.

Jackson, Jennifer. *Ethics in Medicine*. Cambridge: Polity Press, 2006.

James, William. The Moral Philosopher and the Moral Life [1891]. In William James, *The Will to Believe and Other Essays in Popular Philosophy*. New York: Cosimo Classics, 2006: 184–215.

Jarvis, Stephen. Live Long and Die Out: Stephen Jarvis Encounters the Voluntary Human Extinction Movement. *Independent*, April 23, 1994. www.independent.co.uk/life-style/live-long-and-die-out-stephen-jarvis-encounters-the-voluntary-human-extinction-movement-1372200.html.

Johnson, Ben. The Great Horse Manure Crisis of 1894. *Historic UK*. No date. www.historic-uk.com/HistoryUK/HistoryofBritain/Great-Horse-Manure-Crisis-of-1894/.

Jollimore, Troy. Impartiality. In Edward N. Zalta and Uri Nodelman, eds. *The Stanford Encyclopedia of Philosophy*. 2017. https://plato.stanford.edu/archives/fall2017/entries/impartiality/.

Jones, Eric M. "Where Is Everyone?" – An Account of Fermi's Question. *CIC-14 Report Collection*. Los Alamos, NM: National Laboratory, 1985. https://web.archive.org/web/20070629174738/http://www.fas.org/sgp/othergov/doe/lanl/la-10311-ms.pdf.

Kant, Immanuel. *Groundwork of the Metaphysics of Morals* [1785]. Translated and edited by Mary Gregor. Cambridge: Cambridge University Press, 1998. https://cpb-us-w2.wpmucdn.com/blog.nus.edu.sg/dist/c/1868/files/2012/12/Kant-Groundwork-ng0pby.pdf.

Konstan, David. Epicurus. In Edward N. Zalta and Uri Nodelman, eds. *The Stanford Encyclopedia of Philosophy*. 2022. https://plato.stanford.edu/archives/fall2022/entries/epicurus/.

Kraut, Richard. Introduction to the Study of Plato. In Richard Kraut, ed. *The Cambridge Companion to* Plato. Cambridge: Cambridge University Press, 1992: 1–50.

Kraut, Richard. Aristotle's Ethics. In Edward N. Zalta and Uri Nodelman, eds. *The Stanford Encyclopedia of Philosophy*. 2022. https://plato.stanford.edu/archives/fall2022/entries/aristotle-ethics/.

Kurnig. *Der Neo-Nihilismus. Anti-Militarismus. Sexualleben (Ende der Menschheit)*. Leipzig: Verlag Max Sangewald, 1903.

Larousse. Antinataliste. No date. www.larousse.fr/dictionnaires/francais/antinataliste/4164.

Le Guin, Ursula K. The Ones Who Walked Away from Omelas. In Robert Silverberg, ed. *New Dimensions 3*. Garden City, NY: Nelson Doubleday/SFBC, 1973: 1–8. https://shsdavisapes.pbworks.com/f/Omelas.pdf.

Le Robert. Antinataliste. No date. https://dictionnaire.lerobert.com/definition/antinataliste.

Life Sucks. Let's Draw The Cover of Antinatalism Magazine (Jiwoon Hwang and the Ones Who Walk Away From Omelas). Online video clip. June 15, 2019. www.youtube.com/watch?v=i00VQucmXus.

Lochmanová, Kateřina, ed. *History of Antinatalism: How Philosophy Has Challenged the Question of Procreation*. Monee, IL: Kateřina Lochmanová, 2020.

Look, Brandon C. Gottfried Wilhelm Leibniz. In Edward N. Zalta, ed. *The Stanford Encyclopedia of Philosophy*. 2020. https://plato.stanford.edu/archives/spr2020/entries/leibniz/.

Lucretius. *On the Nature of Things*. Translated by Martin Ferguson Smith. Indianapolis, IN: Hackett Publishing Company, 2001.

Maalouf, Amin. *The Crusades through Arab Eyes*. New York: Schocken Books, 1984.

MacCormack, Patricia. *The Ahuman Manifesto: Activism for the End of the Anthropocene*. London: Bloomsbury Academic, 2020.

Magnusson, Erik. On Risk-Based Arguments for Anti-Natalism. *Journal of Value Inquiry* 56 (2022): 101–17.

Malherbe, Abraham J. *The Cynic Epistles: A Study Edition*. Chişinău: Scholars Press, 1977.

Margolis, Rachel, and Myrskylä, Mikko. A Global Perspective on Happiness and Fertility. *Population and Development Review* 37 (2011): 29–56. https://doi.org/10.1111/j.1728-4457.2011.00389.x.

McIntyre, Alison. Doctrine of Double Effect. In Edward N. Zalta, ed. *The Stanford Encyclopedia of Philosophy*. 2019. https://plato.stanford.edu/archives/spr2019/entries/double-effect/.

McKeown, John. *God's Babies: Natalism and Bible Interpretation in Modern America*. Cambridge: Open Book Publishers, 2014.

Metzinger, Thomas. Benevolent Artificial Anti-Natalism (BAAN). *Edge*, July 8, 2017. www.edge.org/conversation/thomas_metzinger-benevolent-artificial-anti-natalism-baan

Meyer, Nicholas. *Star Trek II: The Wrath of Khan*. Online video clip. 1982. www.imdb.com/title/tt0084726/.

Mill, John Stuart. *On Liberty* [1859] *and The Subjection of Women* [1869]. Ware, UK: Wordsworth, 1996.

Miller, Fred. Aristotle's Political Theory. In Edward N. Zalta and Uri Nodelman, eds. *The Stanford Encyclopedia of Philosophy.* 2022. https://plato.stanford.edu/archives/fall2022/entries/aristotle-politics/.

Morioka, Masahiro. *What Is Antinatalism? And Other Essays: Philosophy of Life in Contemporary Society.* Tokyo: Tokyo Philosophy Project, 2021.

Narveson, Jan. Utilitarianism and New Generations. *Mind* 76 (1967): 62–72.

Narveson, Jan. *The Libertarian Idea.* Philadelphia, PA: Temple University Press, 1988.

Nicholson, Reynold Alleyne. *Studies in Islamic Poetry.* Cambridge: Cambridge University Press, 1921. https://ia902602.us.archive.org/4/items/studiesinislamic00nichuoft/studiesinislamic00nichuoft.pdf.

Nietzsche, Friedrich. *The Birth of Tragedy out of the Spirit of Music* [1872]. Edited by Raymond Guess and Ronald Speirs. Translated by Ronald Speirs. Cambridge: Cambridge University Press, 2000.

Oderberg, David S. *Applied Ethics: A Non-Consequentialist Approach.* Oxford: Blackwell, 2000.

Pagels, Elaine. *The Gnostic Gospels.* New York: Random House, 1979.

Parfit, Derek. *Reasons and Persons.* Oxford: Oxford University Press, 1984.

Pasnau, Robert. Thomas Aquinas. In Edward N. Zalta and Uri Nodelman, eds. *The Stanford Encyclopedia of Philosophy.* 2023. https://plato.stanford.edu/archives/spr2023/entries/aquinas/.

Pearce, David. The Hedonistic Imperative. *Hedweb.com.* 1995. www.hedweb.com/.

Pearce, David. What Are the Arguments against Antinatalism? *Quora*, August 22, 2018. https://bit.ly/3TSpCBq.

Plutarch. *Moralia: Volume II. With an English translation by Frank Cole Babbitt.* Cambridge, MA: Harvard University Press, 1928.

Puka, Bill. The Golden Rule. In James Fieser and Bradley Dowden, eds. *Internet Encyclopedia of Philosophy.* No date. https://iep.utm.edu/goldrule/.

Question Mark? Philosophy. EFILism/EFIList Panel ft. @glynos, Oldphan (@anti-natalwolf4449), @LifeSucks, @laithmalekreem6120. Online video clip. May 12, 2021. www.youtube.com/watch?v=zkZuFxcfvCY.

Rist, Rebecca. Did the Cathars Exist? *Readinghistory*, March 6, 2015. https://unireadinghistory.com/2015/03/06/did-the-cathars-exist/.

Rotondo, Andrew. Better to Have Children: A Response to Harrison and Tanner. *Think* 21 (2022): 65–78. https://doi.org/10.1017/S1477175621000348.

Sartre, Jean-Paul. *Nausea* [1938]. Translated by Robert Baldick. London: Penguin Books, 2000.

Savulescu, Julian. Procreative Beneficence: Why We Should Select the Best Children. *Bioethics* 15 (2001): 413–26.

Schopenhauer, Arthur. *Studies In Pessimism: On the Sufferings of the World* [1851]. Translated by Thomas Bailey Sanders [1890]. New York: Cosimo, 2007.

Schultz, Barton. Henry Sidgwick. In Edward N. Zalta, ed. *The Stanford Encyclopedia of Philosophy*. 2021. https://plato.stanford.edu/archives/win2021/entries/sidgwick/.

Scruton, Roger. *A Political Philosophy: Arguments for Conservatism*. London: Continuum, 2006.

Seneca. *On Consolation to Helvia, Marcia, and Polybius: Seneca's Complete Consolations*. Translated by Frank Miller [1917]. Independently published, 2017.

Shead S. Climate Change Is Making People Think Twice about Having Children. *CNBC Sustainable Future*, August 12, 2021. https://bit.ly/3TPddhK.

Shiffrin, Seana Valentine. Wrongful Life, Procreative Responsibility, and the Significance of Harm. *Legal Theory* 5 (1999): 117–48.

Smart, J. J. C., and Williams, Bernard. *Utilitarianism: For and Against*. Cambridge: Cambridge University Press, 1973.

Smart, R. N. Negative Utilitarianism. *Mind* 67 (1958): 542–43.

Sophocles. *The Three Theban Plays: Antigone; Oedipus the King; Oedipus at Colonus*. Translated by Robert Fagles. London: Penguin Classics, 2000.

SufferingSucks. Does Procreation Violate ... [shlockofgod]. Online video clip. October 3, 2011. www.youtube.com/watch?v=2_B_Cwsj-6s.

Sukenick, Amanda. *The EFIList*. 2016. Vimeo film. https://vimeo.com/700934785.

Sukenick, Amanda. Antinatalismquotes. 2023a. www.exploringantinatalism.com/antinatalismquotes/.

Sukenick, Amanda. Biblicalantinatalismquotes. 2023b. www.exploringantinatalism.com/biblicalantinatalismquotes/.

Takala, Tuija. The Child's Right to an Open Future and Modern Genetics. In Brenda Almond and Michael Parker, eds. *Ethical Issues in the New Genetics: Are Genes Us?* Aldershot: Ashgate, 2003: 39–46.

Takala, Tuija, and Häyry, Matti. Justainability. *Cambridge Quarterly of Healthcare Ethics*. Published online June 27, 2023. https://doi.org/10.1017/S0963180123000361.

The Divine Institutes (Lactantius). Translated by William Fletcher. In Alexander Roberts, James Donaldson, and A. Cleveland Coxe, eds. *Ante-Nicene Fathers, Vol. 7*. Buffalo, NY: Christian Literature Publishing, 1886. https://topostext.org/work/543.

The Exploring Antinatalism Podcast #22 – Danny Shine (SocialExperimentalist). Online video clip. November 1, 2020. www.youtube.com/watch?v=0ZFbcs2PLdw.

The Exploring Antinatalism Podcast #57 – Sam Woolfe. Online video clip. April 15, 2022a. www.youtube.com/watch?v=T2TojetQaOc.

The Exploring Antinatalism Podcast #65 – Matti Häyry. Online video clip. September 1, 2022b. www.youtube.com/watch?v=4L1eiDoMuCQ.

The Exploring Antinatalism Podcast #72 – Professor Corey Anton. Online video clip. February 1, 2023. www.youtube.com/watch?v=17wTwMVorVM.

The Graphene Rule. The Vegan Antinatalist Connection. Online video clip. March 8, 2020. www.youtube.com/watch?v=n998MZqmkUI.

The Voluntary Human Extinction Movement. Website. 1996. www.vhemt.org/.

Tornau, Christian. Saint Augustine. In Edward N. Zalta, ed. *The Stanford Encyclopedia of Philosophy*. 2020. https://plato.stanford.edu/archives/sum2020/entries/augustine/.

Tremain, Shelley. Dialogues on Disability: Shelley Tremain Interviews Christine Overall. *Biopolitical Philosophy*, June 16, 2021. https://bit.ly/47rt5dn.

Warren, James. *Facing Death: Epicurus and His Critics*. Oxford: Clarendon Press, 2004.

Weinberg, Rivka. *The Risk of a Lifetime: How, When, and Why Procreation May Be Permissible*. Oxford: Oxford University Press, 2016.

Williams Alex. To Breed or Not to breed? *New York Times*, November 20, 2021. www.nytimes.com/2021/11/20/style/breed-children-climate-change.html.

Williams, Garrath. Kant's Account of Reason. In Edward N. Zalta and Uri Nodelman, eds. *The Stanford Encyclopedia of Philosophy*. 2023. https://plato.stanford.edu/entries/kant-reason/.

Wilson, Kenneth M. *Augustine's Conversion from Traditional Free Choice to "Non-free Free Will": A Comprehensive Methodology*. Tübingen: Mohr Siebeck, 2018.

Woolfe, Sam. The Ones Who Walk Away from Omelas by Ursula K. Le Guin: An Analogy for Antinatalism. Published online June 15, 2020. www.samwoolfe.com/2020/06/the-ones-who-walk-away-from-omelas-antinatalism.html.

Yarbrough, O. Larry. *Not Like the Gentiles: Marriage Rules in the Letters of Paul*. Atlanta. GA: Scholars Press, 1986.

Zapffe, Peter Wessel. The Last Messiah [1933]. Translated by Gisle R. Tangenes. *Philosophy Now* 45, March/April 2004. https://philosophynow.org/issues/45/The_Last_Messiah.

Acknowledgments

Our sincere thanks are due to Anugrah Kumar, Lawrence Anton, Danny Shine, Elizabeth Barber, Julio Cabrera, Karim Akerma, Lucas Fajardo, Mike Fontaine, and Tim Oseckas for their warm and expert support.

Cambridge Elements

Bioethics and Neuroethics

Thomasine Kushner
California Pacific Medical Center, San Francisco

Thomasine Kushner, PhD, is the founding Editor of the *Cambridge Quarterly of Healthcare Ethics* and coordinates the International Bioethics Retreat, where bioethicists share their current research projects, the Cambridge Consortium for Bioethics Education, a growing network of global bioethics educators, and the Cambridge-ICM Neuroethics Network, which provides a setting for leading brain scientists and ethicists to learn from each other.

About the Series

Bioethics and neuroethics play pivotal roles in today's debates in philosophy, science, law, and health policy. With the rapid growth of scientific and technological advances, their importance will only increase. This series provides focused and comprehensive coverage in both disciplines consisting of foundational topics, current subjects under discussion and views toward future developments.

Cambridge Elements

Bioethics and Neuroethics

Elements in the Series

The Ethics of Consciousness
Walter Glannon

Responsibility for Health
Sven Ove Hansson

Roles of Justice in Bioethics
Matti Häyry

Bioethics, Public Reason, and Religion: The Liberalism Problem
Leonard M. Fleck

Controlling Love: The Ethics and Desirability of Using 'Love Drugs'
Peter Herissone-Kelly

Pathographies of Mental Illness
Nathan Carlin

Immune Ethics
Walter Glannon

What Placebos Teach Us about Health and Care: A Philosopher Pops a Pill
Dien Ho

The Methods of Neuroethics
Luca Malatesti and John McMillan

Philosophical, Medical, and Legal Controversies About Brain Death
L. Syd M Johnson

Antinatalism, Extinction, and the End of Procreative Self-Corruption
Matti Häyry and Amanda Sukenick

A full series listing is available at: www.cambridge.org/EBAN